INSIDE CONTENT MARKETING

ECONTENT MAGAZINE'S GUIDE TO ROLES, TOOLS, AND STRATEGIES FOR THRIVING IN THE AGE OF BRAND JOURNALISM

THERESA CRAMER

Medford, New Jersey

Information Today, Inc.

First printing

Inside Content Marketing:* EContent *Magazine's Guide to Roles, Tools, and Strategies for Thriving in the Age of Brand Journalism

Library of Congress Cataloging-in-Publication Data

Names: Cramer, Theresa, 1981- author.
Title: Inside content marketing : econtent magazine's guide to roles, tools, and strategies for thriving in the age of brand journalism / Theresa Cramer.
Description: Medford, New Jersey : Information Today, Inc., 2016. | Includes index.
Identifiers: LCCN 2015051390 | ISBN 9781937290061 (paperback)
Subjects: LCSH: Internet marketing. | Online social networks. | BISAC: BUSINESS & ECONOMICS / Marketing / General. | BUSINESS & ECONOMICS / General.
Classification: LCC HF5415.1265 .C73 2016 | DDC 658.8/72—dc23
LC record available at http://lccn.loc.gov/2015051390

Printed and bound in the United States of America

President and CEO: Thomas H. Hogan, Sr.
Editor-in-Chief and Publisher: John B. Bryans
Associate Editor: Patricia Robinson
Production Manager: Tiffany Chamenko
Marketing Coordinator: Rob Colding
Indexer: Kathleen Rocheleau

Composition by Amnet Systems

infotoday.com

For Nana and Papa.
Thanks for everything.

Praise for *Inside Content Marketing*

"Where *Inside Content Marketing* departs from an endless sea of content marketing books and blogs is the deep analysis and insight into the content marketing/journalism connection. Debunking the notion that branded content means working for the 'dark side,' Theresa Cramer shines light on an emerging world in which brand publishers and journalists alike collaborate to produce meaningful content that connects, both intellectually and emotionally."

—Russell Sparkman, CEO, FusionSpark Media

"The road to great content marketing is full of wrong turns and dead ends for both marketers and journalists—with Theresa Cramer's engrossing new guide, we now have a map."

—Sam Slaughter, VP Content, Contently

"Content marketing might seem like solely the domain of the marketing department. But the smartest companies know that it's actually a collaborative effort. Theresa Cramer tells you why—and she lays out the prescription for how to vastly increase the success of your own program."

—Ann Handley, Chief Content Officer, MarketingProfs

"In the land of the blind, the one-eyed man is King. Theresa Cramer is the one-eyed Queen in the land of the content marketing blind—which is all of the rest of us."

—Tim Bourgeois, Founder, ChiefDigitalOfficer.net

"There are many ways to generate attention for your product, service, personal brand, or cause. Nearly all require spending boatloads of money on agencies and advertising. Theresa Cramer shows you how content marketing has evolved into the best way to get your ideas out there to grow your business. And it's all free!"

—David Meerman Scott, *The New Rules of Marketing and PR*

Contents

Part III: Publishers and the Custom Content Boom

Acknowledgments

The idea of thanking all of the people who helped contribute to *Inside Content Marketing* is overwhelming. First, I must express profound gratitude for my family; especially my parents, Tammy and Dave, who will surely be telling everyone they know about this book, but also my brother and extended family of aunts, uncles, cousins, and grandparents. They keep me grounded and provide the kind of support we all need to succeed.

I also have to thank Michelle Manafy. She hired me as an assistant editor at *EContent* so many years ago and helped get me started on the path that led me here. And more often than not, she provided a sounding board to help me talk through my ideas. She also offered me valuable feedback on this book, as did Allison Foster. Thanks also goes to Brian Chevalier, whose belief that with a lot of effort—and caffeine—we can all accomplish anything we can imagine gave me the push I needed to write the book.

I would be remiss not to mention Ruby, my cat, whose bout with gallstones and the associated veterinary bills forced me to stop procrastinating, and ultimately led to me finally pitching a book idea that I'd been tossing around for months.

And that brings me to my editor, John B. Bryans, who believed in this project from the first email I sent to test the waters. Without him and the rest of the Information Today, Inc. crew, *Inside Content Marketing* would not have happened.

And of course there are the many people who consented to be interviewed and lend their ideas and knowledge to the book. Their expertise is what will make it a success.

Introduction

One day I found myself sitting at my desk weeping at a video that popped up in my Facebook feed. This happens fairly frequently, so that wasn't what surprised me. It was a short film on Vimeo made by a photographer from the point of view of his dying dog. *Denali* was a beautiful ode to the bond between a man and his best friend, both of whom had lived pretty amazing lives. Beautiful footage from one last day at the beach interspersed with photographs from their 14 years together showed one adventure after another—including the filmmaker's bout with colon cancer and the dog's determination to stay by his side.

The two friends surfed, rock climbed, and hiked all over the country together—even after the battle with cancer. As sad as it was, the movie was also funny, but it was the credits that really surprised me. This wonderful little film—which had me hugging my dog so close she probably thought I'd lost my mind—had been "Made Possible by Patagonia." There were also a handful of other, smaller sponsors in there.

I thought back for a minute to one picture that had caught my attention. It was of Denali curled up at camp with a Patagonia jacket draped over him to keep him warm. In that moment I'd thought, "If Patagonia didn't sponsor this, they really missed the boat." Other than the occasional (completely organic and authentic) appearance of a sponsor's product, there were no brand mentions. Nonetheless, I resolved that my next winter coat will be from Patagonia.

I watched over the next few days and weeks as my friends shared the video on social media. I clicked on it each time and was moved to tears all over again. Why isn't all content marketing this good? Why aren't we all weeping, or laughing hysterically, or emphatically shaking our heads in agreement with every piece of content marketing that crosses our path? Why isn't every brand so in tune with its audience that all of its content elicits as strong a response as *Denali*?

All of those questions can be distilled into one that I kept in mind while writing this book: "What is the biggest obstacle to content marketing success?" Some will tell you that a lack of strategy is at the heart of many marketers' problems. There is plenty of truth to that—and *Inside Content Marketing* will certainly cover the necessity of a documented strategy—but I think there is a fundamental lack of understanding that haunts many marketing departments. Many still don't understand exactly what creating great content marketing entails.

Content creation is a collaborative process. It takes a team of people who know how to conceive of, create, deliver, and promote quality content that will delight audiences—and this book is written for all the members of that team. Especially the reluctant ones.

In the new world of brand journalism, everyone needs to reevaluate their place in the content ecosystem. Marketers have to think like journalists. Journalists have to understand marketers. And publishers have to bring everyone together. These are not small tasks.

Marketers will be first to the content marketing table. In fact, they are already there, eager to implement this new engagement tactic to capture customers' attention. Selling is in their blood, and it will be difficult—if not impossible—for many of them to leave the marketing mindset behind and start thinking like a storyteller. That's where journalists come in.

Journalists, however, have been the most reluctant to embrace content marketing. Concerned by issues of editorial integrity, many journalists still eschew this new career path (although plenty of them *are* embracing it and you'll hear from them in the book). It's up to marketers—and publishers—to help journalists understand that they need neither compromise their ethics nor sacrifice their creativity in taking on content marketing work.

Publishers, on the other hand, should be jumping at the chance to help advertisers create branded content! Would you, under any other circumstance, refuse to use your expertise and platform to help your advertisers reach their audience? I doubt it. Yet many publishers are still letting this revenue stream pass them by.

Marketers. Journalists. Publishers. These are the people at the crux of content marketing. It behooves them to understand where they all fit in the value chain, and how, by working together, they can help this industry to continue to thrive. Perhaps just as important as understanding their own place in the world of content marketing is understanding their colleagues. If marketers could help assuage the fears of journalists, and journalists could understand what marketers truly need from content, the end result would be a product everyone is proud of. Publishers can help bring these two groups together—and profit in the process.

Inside Content Marketing is broken up into three parts: the first focuses on the marketer's experience, and what they need to know to create *Denali*-level content; the second makes the case for content marketing to journalists; the third helps publishers understand how they can capitalize on this shift in the marketing industry—and explains why marketers should be teaming up with publishers who already have an audience, and storytelling experience. While you may be tempted to go straight to the section of the book that speaks most directly to you, that would be a mistake. Creating the kind of content that audiences want is a team sport. Understanding your teammates—and the very important roles you all play in the game—is a crucial part of creating the kind of content that audiences crave and brings them back to your brand time and again.

In this book you will find practical advice on how to create meaningful content marketing strategies, hear from the experts on some of the most challenging aspects of the practice, and delve into some of the best examples of content marketing the world has to offer. You will also hear from people working in every corner of content marketing, and gain invaluable knowledge about bringing together a content marketing dream team that can turn your brand into a rock star!

Part I

The Marketer's Mission

Chapter 1

What *Is* Content Marketing, Really?

When you think about marketing, what do you picture? Flyers? Coupons? Billboards? Banner ads? Or do you picture a white paper, a blog post, or an infographic? If you picture the latter, then it's safe to say you are part of the content marketing revolution. Consumer expectations are changing and so are the tactics companies are using to reach them. Today's customers are looking for more than a few dollars off, and today's marketers are giving consumers the information and value they need through content marketing.

Study after study confirms what most of us already know: People respond to content, not advertising. According to "Consumers' Attitudes Toward Custom Content," 70 percent of people surveyed say they "prefer to learn about a company through a collection of articles rather than in an ad." Marketers have heard that message loud and clear, embracing the idea of content marketing wholeheartedly. The interest in content marketing has only grown since that study came out, as audiences have become even more discerning about the content they consume.

However, if you believe the numbers (and I am about to share a lot of numbers with you), you probably don't need convincing that content marketing is a must-have tool in your bag of marketing tricks. Google searches for the term "content marketing" have grown 400 percent since 2011. Back in 2014, the Content Marketing Institute (CMI) and MarketingProfs found that 93 percent of marketers said they were using content marketing. That number is so high it's almost shocking. In 2015, they tweaked the definition of content marketing and got slightly different results, with 86 percent of respondents saying their organizations use content marketing. In 2016 that number jumped a bit to 88 percent. It's clear that the siren song of content marketing is strong, and if you aren't careful about your approach, you might just crash on the rocks.

At first glance, content marketing seems simple—almost a dream come true. Instead of buying expensive billboards or television ads to raise brand awareness, all you have to do is create some great content, post it on your blog, promote it through your social channels, and *voila!* Right?

Wrong.

While traditional marketers and brands may be eager to cash in on the content marketing craze, I have a word of warning for them: Content marketing isn't as easy as it seems. According to CMI's *B2C Content Marketing 2016 Benchmarks, Budgets, and Trends—North America,* 76 percent of Business to Consumer (B2C) marketers are using content marketing but only 28 percent consider themselves effective at it (with just 10 percent describing themselves as very effective). That hasn't slowed down the content machine, though. The amount of content companies continue to create has grown consistently—even though only 43 percent understand what "content marketing success" looks like. Here's the takeaway: The buzz is massive, but many still struggle to define content marketing, let alone implement it successfully.

Social Media Today's "13 Ways Content Marketers Miss the Mark" found that the three biggest complaints expressed by B2B audiences are too many barriers to downloading materials, self-promotional content, and (perhaps the worst offense of all) content that lacks substance. While it is tempting to dismiss the marketers creating this content as a clueless minority, it's clear that a hefty majority of marketers and brands are still struggling to fine-tune their content marketing and make it a useful part of their overall strategy. Forrester's "Compare Your B2B Content Marketing Maturity" found that "51 percent of B2B marketing leaders rate their content marketing practices as very mature, an overwhelming 85 percent fail to connect content activity to business value—and, as a result, fail to retain customers or win their long-term loyalty." These results are unacceptable—especially for a channel that is so important to so many companies—but they are also predictable, considering that so many practitioners still don't grasp the real meaning of content marketing.

Defining Content Marketing

So let's start at the beginning by simply defining what content marketing is. If you ask 100 different people, you're likely to get 100 different answers. The confusion stems in part from the stealthy nature of content marketing, which aims to go (almost) unnoticed as marketing while simultaneously providing valuable content to customers that ultimately raises the brand's profile and results in sales.

> "Content marketing is a blanket term that describes the process of creating and sharing relevant brand information in hopes of engaging current consumers and attracting new ones. Also referred to as branded content and custom publishing, in the internet age, content marketing is the act of relaying this valuable information. ... Content marketers believe that sharing specialized content leads to a better informed consumer, and a better informed consumer yields more profitable results."
>
> *Eileen Mullan, "What Is Content Marketing?" (EContentmag.com)*

Unlike so many other things in life, you may not know content marketing when you see it. In fact, if the content creators are doing their jobs right, you often won't notice you're being marketed to until it's too late, and you're already poking around the brand's site—or are even in a store—to purchase the product the marketers were hoping you would buy all along. To complicate matters further, content marketing often doesn't even reveal what it's selling. Take, for instance, Chipotle's *Farmed and Dangerous* (see Figure 1.1), a show the burrito-slinging chain created for Hulu.

Antony Young described the show on Adage.com: "*Farmed and Dangerous* takes branded content to another level by not including any branding at all in the show. Social Media Week organizers dubbed it Unbranded Entertainment. Chipotle and other advertisers placed commercials in the show, but by not including branding in

Figure 1.1 A screenshot of *Farmed and Dangerous,* an original series by Chipotle that ran on Hulu.

the show itself, the restaurant has taken a risk that few marketers would entertain."

Instead of pushing burritos, *Farmed and Dangerous* used comedy to reach the masses with a message from Chipotle—though viewers may have been blissfully unaware where the content was coming from. Famous for its efforts to source ingredients sustainably, Chipotle created a show about the dangers of industrial agriculture, not about its own food.

This wasn't the first time Chipotle tackled this topic in its marketing. Many may remember its "Back to the Start Commercial" that featured Willie Nelson singing Coldplay's "The Scientist" while adorable animated farmers realized the error of their industrialized ways. If you didn't watch carefully, you may have missed the Chipotle tag at the end.

Not all content marketing will be devoid of any branding. In fact, if your goal is to drive actual sales and not just general "brand lift," then you will almost certainly have to include some brand information, but it's important to keep one thing in mind: Your content should aim to answer a question for your potential customers; promoting your brand must always be secondary to that mission. Chipotle understands this and takes it very seriously.

More recently, Chipotle won a PR Award at Cannes for a 3½–minute video about a scarecrow that is disillusioned with the food system but finds happiness through serving burrito bowls filled

> "Content marketing is a strategic marketing approach focused on creating and distributing valuable, relevant, and consistent content to attract and retain a clearly defined audience—and, ultimately, to drive profitable customer action."
>
> *What Is Content Marketing? (Content Marketing Institute)*

with fresh ingredients to customers (see Figure 1.2). More importantly, the video was a companion piece for a game—delivered in app form—that continued Chipotle's content marketing mission of promoting sustainable food practices.

With so many different formats, channels, and mediums available to content marketers—video, apps, blogs, feature films, and beyond—you can see how a newbie might be a bit confused about how to get a successful content marketing effort up and running. According to CMI's 2016 B2C research, "This year, [content marketers are] allocating 32% of their total marketing budget, on average, to content marketing (vs. 25% last year)." With numbers like that, it's essential that marketers start getting their content marketing strategies right.

It doesn't have to be confusing. "At its very core [good content marketing is] delivery of value that goes beyond the product or service being marketed," says Robert Rose, chief strategist at CMI. "Great content marketing can stand on its own—and delivers education, entertainment, and engagement without the need of the product or service. That's really the litmus test. If the content would stand by itself as a valuable experience (because of, or even despite the brand's involvement) to a consumer—then it's great content marketing."

Creating a memorable ad is hard enough, but creating the kind of content Rose describes seems to be damn near impossible for many marketers. At the Cannes International Festival of Creativity in 2015, there was no Grand Prix winner in the branded content and entertainment category. Not only are marketers falling short of

Figure 1.2 A screenshot of "The Scarecrow," an award-winning video from Chipotle.

their own goals but their content literally isn't winning any prizes for creativity. There are plenty of reasons for this—which we'll explore in these pages—but one thing seems clear: Many marketers still don't "get it."

What Are Marketers Doing Wrong?

The Content Marketing Institute delved deeper into the numbers in its *2014 Benchmarks, Budgets, and Trends* report, looking at what made the organizations that were confident in their content marketing successful. A couple of things stood out. A hefty majority—60 percent—of the companies that rated their efforts highly had a documented content strategy, as opposed to just 12 percent of the least effective. Additionally, 85 percent of the strongest marketers had "someone who oversees content marketing strategy" in comparison to 50 percent of the least effective.

The 2015 version of the report supported these findings but looked at the numbers a bit differently. The report found that "most B2B marketers have a content marketing strategy—but only 35 percent have documented it" according to a post on the CMI site (see Figure 1.3). By 2016, that number had shrunk to just 32 percent. This

> ***EContent:*** *What do you think is the most significant challenge that content marketing is facing today?*
>
> **Joe Pulizzi:** It's different than what most companies are used to. The practice of content marketing is not necessarily rocket science, but it's significantly different than how most organizations are set up. Change is hard, especially in big companies. Agile companies and even startups have an easier time with content marketing than longstanding companies because of this. We believe that education and training is the way to break through to these organizations. Well, I don't know of a better way.
>
> *Excerpted from "Q&A: Joe Pulizzi, Founder, Content Marketing Institute" (EContentmag.com)*

presents some problems. "B2B marketers who have a documented strategy are more effective and less challenged with every aspect of content marketing when compared with their peers who only have a verbal strategy or no strategy at all," says the CMI post.

It's clear that two of the secrets to content marketing success are planning and oversight, but not everyone is getting that message. The low barrier to entry and deceptively simple tactics of content marketing can be misleading for those who don't understand the need for a coherent strategy, or simply don't understand what one looks like. As Greg Satell wrote on Forbes.com, "Alas, I discovered that content strategy was in reality just another name for brand planners selling long form ads to clients. Nobody who was talking about content strategy seemed to have ever published or produced anything." (That is why organizations should hire a journalist, but we'll get to that later.) Creating a meaningful content marketing strategy, and holding your staff accountable for achieving the goals set out by the strategy, are important to any endeavor, and that is no different when it comes to creating branded content.

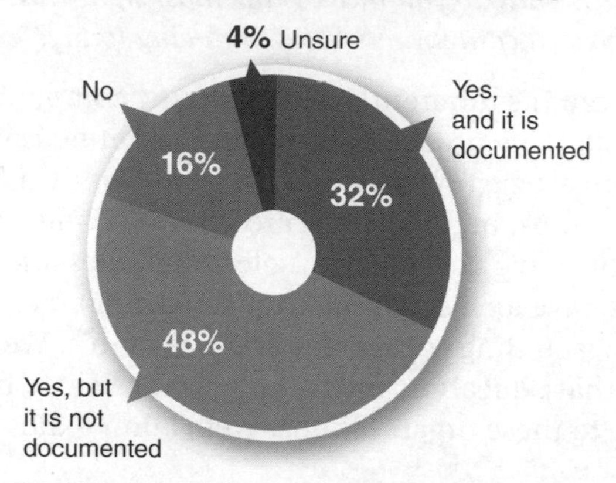

Figure 1.3 A chart from Content Marketing Institute that says only 32% of companies have a documented content marketing strategy in 2016.

However, if developing a content marketing strategy were as easy as it sounds, so many companies would not still be struggling with it. In fact, IMN's 2014 Content Marketing Survey reported that 30 percent of its respondents admitted to "winging it" when it came to their strategy. Joe Pulizzi, founder of CMI, suggested in his "7 Content Marketing Strategies for 2013"column for *EContent* that a mission statement might be a good place to start. Pulizzi wrote:

"I've surveyed about 1,000 people over the past month, asking each if they have developed an editorial mission, or content marketing mission statement, for their content strategies. Easily less than 5% had something like this prepared, let alone a content marketing strategy.

"This is a major problem. How can we execute a content strategy if we don't have a clear vision for why we are developing the content in the first place?

"Every person that touches the content marketing program should know, by heart, what the mission of the content strategy is. In addition, if you don't have a content vision, how do you know which stories should or should not be included? This is a major problem."

But what does a truly meaningful mission statement consist of? According to Rose, there are three questions that need to be addressed:

1. Who is the intended audience?
2. What value will be delivered in the content?
3. How will the audience be better off having experienced the content?

I would also add that you should begin to address your own goals with your mission statement. It's never too early to define what you consider success so that you'll be able to measure your return on investment (ROI) later.

Once you understand why you are creating content, you'll be able to better detail and execute your strategy—but even the folks at CMI have had trouble battling the content strategy demons. As Robert Rose wrote in a CMI post about the difference between content marketing and content strategy, "But, here at CMI we haven't yet (at least, not to the extent that we should) fully embraced the advancement of content strategy, or helped preach the distinction between the skill sets needed for content marketing and those required for content strategy. In fact, we've been guilty of using the terms 'content marketing strategy' and 'content strategy' interchangeably at times (we have resolved to be more clear on this, moving forward)."

The experts at CMI aren't the only ones conflating content strategy and content marketing—to say nothing of content marketing strategy. A few years ago, I was being interviewed and the writer asked me what, if any, difference there was between content marketing and content strategy. I was confused for a moment. In a way, I didn't even understand the question. My background in journalism and publishing—not marketing—had led me to distinguish between these two things long before anyone else seemed to have. Eventually I pulled myself together and said something like, "These are two completely different concepts but you can't be successful at one (content marketing) without the other (content strategy)." It wasn't until Rose's *mea culpa* that I realized this was a common misconception—and eventually had both Rose and "Content Wrangler" Scott Abel on an *EContent* Live Hangout to hash out the difference between content strategy and content marketing once and for all.

For the record, content strategy is, at least according to Kristina Halvorson, author of *Content Strategy for the Web,* "Planning for the creation, delivery, and governance of useful, usable content." (Really smart marketers will add "measurement" to that list—because you always need to know what's working.)

Content Strategy vs. Content Marketing Strategy

"Well there are two different things at play here—a content strategy and a content marketing strategy," says Rose. "I view them as different. Related, but different. A content strategy is the holistic approach to managing content in an organization. It is how we organize, manage, and utilize content as a strategic asset. So it covers all manner of content—from the documentation of our products, to our customer onboarding forms, to our invoicing terminology to the way we communicate and so on and so on. Content marketing strategy, on the other hand, is solely devoted to the practice of how we use content to drive a marketing-related business purpose."

He continues: "The content marketing strategy is narrower in scope, certainly, and truly focuses how we use that created value in order to differentiate our offering, create reasons for customers to become customers, and ultimately create loyalty and evangelism among our constituents."

The moral of the story is that even the experts get it wrong sometimes, and if you're planning on making content marketing part of your repertoire, it's important to not only have a clear mission statement for your content objectives but also to make sure you have an overarching strategy in place to govern your every move. One of the keys to creating and implementing that strategy will be finding the right people.

The Chief Content Marketing Officer to the Rescue

You may recall that one of the factors cited by successful content marketers is having "someone who oversees content marketing strategy." Yes, accountability is key. According to Curata's "Content Marketing Tactics Planner," 71 percent of companies plan on increasing content marketing budgets, and the same study found that the bulk of that money is going toward money and people. At the time, 57 percent said they did not have an executive directly responsible for content marketing, and that while new sales and leads were the top goals of most content marketing campaigns, companies found their efforts had more impact on brand awareness. Curata's chief marketing officer, Michael Gerard, told *EContent* he thought the lack of oversight might be why goals and results weren't matching up.

"Getting the organization to invest in a new role, content marketing executive, who will coalesce all of the content-related resources across the organization is no easy feat," Gerard said. "From a tactical perspective, content marketing requires a detailed understanding of the digital marketing space. Many marketing executives continue to struggle to keep up-to-date with this rapidly developing space while dealing with the everyday pressures of managing a large marketing organization."

According to "The Rise of the Chief Content Officer" by Bill Kolbenschlag, Petco, Netflix, and Coca-Cola all have chief content officers or a similar position. Before long, hiring a content officer will be unavoidable even for smaller companies—at least if they hope to ever be successful. What exactly will that new position be doing? "This is hard to say definitively because of the varying degrees of role that this person plays," says Rose. "But ideally, they are the chief storyteller for the organization. They are responsible for managing content as a strategic asset for marketing and communications."

Pulizzi has a slightly different take. He says you will need "someone with a clear understanding of your audience, combined with someone who can execute consistent stories. This could be a journalist, editor, copywriter, producer, broadcaster—most likely someone who has worked with the media. If we are positioning ourselves as publishers, we need to search out and find talent with media savvy and experience."

Finding the right person to be in charge of your content marketing efforts may not be easy, but one thing should be clear: You probably don't want that person to be a marketer, because the emphasis should always be on the content.

The Building Blocks of Good Content Marketing

Now that we have defined content marketing, cleared up the content marketing vs. content strategy confusion, and you know you need to start looking for someone to oversee your content marketing efforts, you might be wondering what good content marketing looks like. We'll look at specific examples later; for now, let's talk about the basics.

For this I turned to the experts. Joe Pulizzi offered the following list of six elements that are essential to "dominating your niche with content."

1. Your content *must fill an audience need* in some way.
2. *Consistency wins.* Content marketing is not a campaign.
3. *Write/Create/Produce like a human.* Remove all corporate speak.
4. *Have a point of view.* What's your take? Become the thought leader.
5. *Remove the sale from your content.* Inserting product and sales messages in your content will kill your strategy.
6. *Be best of breed.* To win it, you need to set a goal to be the leading informational provider in your industry niche.

These are clear, simple goals. Now let's figure out how to achieve them, and what they look like in practice.

Filling the Audience Need

It should go without saying that your content must address a need for your audience, though this seems to be one of the hardest lessons for marketers to learn. Content is not about the organization, its products, or services—it's about customers and prospects. Answer their questions. Address their concerns. Entertain them. Just give them the content they want.

The energy drink company Red Bull is a legend in the content marketing industry. Recognizing that no one was catering to extreme sports enthusiasts, it filled the gap with a variety of content aimed at that underserved audience. In the process, it won a legion of new fans and grew to become one of the biggest energy drink companies in the world.

The Importance of Consistency

As Joe Pulizzi says, content marketing is not a campaign. Rather, it is a sustained part of your overall marketing strategy. You can't expect to post on your blog now and then or tweet an infographic every few months and find success. To truly gain your customers' trust and build a relationship based on addressing their needs, you need to be consistent. Just like a traditional media outlet, it's important to let your audience know what kind of content to expect from you and how often to expect it, and you will establish a relationship that has your users seeking out your content. Don't forget, it's not just about making the sale, it's about retaining that customer and making him a loyal brand advocate, and that means you're in it for the long haul.

Humanize Your Content

No one likes content packed with keywords and industry jargon—not even Google. While it is certainly important to create clear, concise content that, ideally, can be repurposed for other formats and uses, it's important to remember that you are connecting with people, not machines. For starters, creating an interesting and compelling social media presence helps customers get to know "the real you." On a more granular level, replacing a sterile sales pitch with a real-life scenario can put a human face on a problem and help prospects intuitively grasp what you have to offer them.

Thought Leadership

Let's be clear about one thing: There is no shortage of content. We are all competing for the limited attention of the same group of consumers, which is why it's important to stand out among the crowd as not only a provider of great content but as a thought leader. That means you can't be content to rehash the same old ideas and serve them up in a different package. You need to say something new, have a clear point of view, and make sure your voice is *the* authority. That may mean thinking beyond the written word, videos, and other tricks of the marketing trade. Maybe your CEO needs to hit the lecture circuit or put out an ebook. Those are the details only you can decide on, but whatever you decide, you need to shake things up and make your voice heard.

Banish the Sales Pitch

If there is one thing you take away from this book—and, of course, I hope you absorb more than that—it should be that content marketing is not about making a sales pitch. If you find yourself tempted to start name-dropping your products and urging readers to contact your sales department, think again. Please refer back to "Filling the Audience Need" if you're confused about what you *should* be doing with your content marketing. Establish yourself as a trusted source of knowledge and sales will eventually follow. If you try to force it, you'll lose the audience's confidence.

Be the Best

I've said it before and I'll say it again—there is no shortage of content. To stand out, therefore, your content marketing needs to be better than the rest. Your research needs to be deeper; your blog posts need to be funnier and more informative; your videos need to be more entertaining; and your ideas need to be more cutting edge. You need to be organized and have a very clear mission. You aren't just competing with your normal competitors here—you're up against every media outlet and content source on the web, and you need to make your voice heard above the din.

You Get What You Measure

Of course, all the strategy and talent in the world won't get you anywhere if you're not aiming for the right goals and taking the right measurements. After all, for most brands, the aim is to use content marketing to win new customers and retain existing ones, and to

Reaching Millennials

It's no secret that millennials have almost no brand loyalty but still represent massive buying power and social media cachet. According to *Content Marketing: Best Practices Among Millennials,* a report from Yahoo!, Tumblr, Razorfish, and Digitas, 45 percent of millennials don't find content marketing compelling enough to share. The report identified the following five strategic principles to help brands better engage the digital native demographic.

1. **"Be Native, Not Deceptive."** The report found that millennials are willing to share advertising, but it has to be relevant and cannot aim to deceive the reader in any way.
2. **"Be an Individual...And Be Ready to Evolve."** Millennials respond to personality. They want to get to know a brand and to see that brand strive to stay culturally relevant.
3. **"Deliver on an Emotion...And Know That Humor Rules."** Millennials like funny content, no matter what form it comes in. Humor rules online, but if you can succeed at making a digital native feel *any* emotion, you will be rewarded.
4. **"Reserve Judgment."** Millennials aren't interested in your judgment and hang-ups. Self-expression is important to them, even in interactions with brands.
5. **"Act Like the Locals."** Millennials are all over the internet. They know the ins and outs of all their favorite sites and they expect you to as well. That includes being familiar with and using all the appropriate formats, whether it's a six-second video or a 140-character tweet.

do that you need information. CMI found in its *B2B Content Marketing: 2015 Benchmarks, Budgets, and Trends—North America* that most marketers are using website traffic to measure their success. This is a recurring trend, and it's one that Joe Pulizzi finds troubling. He says that growing your subscriber list should be the goal. Why? Because getting subscriber information allows you to understand more about the people using your content and to ultimately deliver the right content to further cultivate your relationship. In other words, it's all about the leads.

Still, CMI also found that only 21 percent of respondents say they are successful at tracking ROI. Having a strategy helps—the number jumps to 35 percent for marketers who have one—but getting the desired results remains elusive for many.

While 63 percent of respondents said they use website traffic to measure their content marketing success, only 30 percent cited subscriber growth. Sales lead quality, higher conversion rates, sales, sales lead quantity, search engine optimization (SEO) ranking, time spent on site, inbound links, and qualitative feedback from customers were also on the list. That's a lot of factors to take into account, but there's a reason Pulizzi advocates for new subscriptions. You don't want your content to be a thinly veiled sales pitch for your widgets, but if you can encourage readers to sign up for, say, a newsletter, you can parlay the information you gain—and the access you've earned—into things like sales and higher conversion rates by nurturing the relationship with great content. Once you have someone's name and information, it's easier to track them through the rest of the sales funnel.

Jay Baer offers useful insight into the world of measurement in "The 4 Types of Content Metrics That Matter" on Convince and Convert. According to Baer, "Content cannot be measured with a single metric, because no one data point can successfully or satisfactorily tell you whether your program is working. Instead, you need to create an array of metrics that are selected from four primary buckets..." He goes on to list consumption metrics, sharing metrics, lead generation metrics, and sales metrics as the four numbers marketers need to be looking at to ensure they are getting the desired results.

According to Cody Goolsby's post "The Four Fundamentals of Reporting Inbound Marketing Progress" on Business2Community .com, there are four "pillars" to consider when setting your budget and evaluating content marketing success:

1. **Goals.** "You can only measure ROI against established goals. Make certain everyone knows what they are!"
2. **Key Performance Indicators (KPIs).** "The KPIs you choose should have a direct correlation to your goals."
3. **Closed Loop Marketing.** "Closed loop marketing happens when your sales team reports back to your marketing team with the results from the leads they generated."
4. **Reports Need to Be Actionable.** "By looking at your KPIs, you should be able to formulate actionable items to improve your ROI."

These benchmarks should sound familiar to marketers but, for reasons that still escape me, they go ignored among many content marketers. I do have a theory about why so many content marketers still have trouble reaching their goals, and it comes down to a case of mixed messaging.

Mixed Messages and Measurement

I realize that, sometimes, the messages coming from content marketing experts can seem contradictory. Don't fill your content with sales pitches, but don't forget it's all about the sale. Confusing, right? It's no wonder so many brands end up missing their content marketing goals. All of a sudden, it's more understandable why marketers are seeing plenty of brand lift but not enough new sales leads. How do you create great content that isn't too "salesy," but can still convert readers to customers, while at the same time being able to prove the content worked?

Jordan Berg wrote "Opinion: Five Ways to Measure Your Content Marketing" for Digiday, and a couple of his suggestions addressed this very issue. His first point that stands out for me is, "Don't simply create content. Create content campaigns."

This goes back to the need for consistency. Imagine that your goal is to sell more widgets to women aged 30–35. You start by creating an infographic and sharing it with your social channels. You see that the topic is popular with your target audience—through sharing metrics, new likes, and followers—so you write a longer, more informative blog post on the topic and share it. This time, however, you include a link to your newsletter sign-up. Now you have a more direct connection to the women you are trying to reach, and a lot more information about them. You can craft newsletters filled with original and curated content that will interest your readers, and eventually you can include a call to action with a specialized landing page that will make it easy for you to see how effectively your content campaign is converting readers to customers. And, after those customers make purchases, you can continue to nurture the relationships with helpful tips and tricks on how to use your widget.

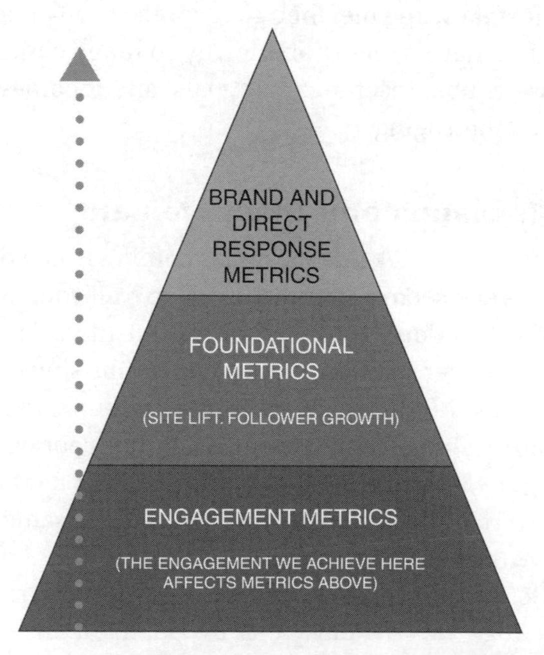

Figure 1.4 Jordan Berg, founding partner of Questus, created the Analytics Pyramid (reprinted with permission of Jordan Berg).

Berg puts this a bit more succinctly, writing that "Engagement metrics drive brand metrics." He also describes an analytics pyramid with engagement metrics at the bottom (see Figure 1.4), which then lead to more foundational metrics (such as site traffic and follower growth). At the top of the pyramid is brand and direct response metrics.

Just remember that you have to start with sound goals and develop the right strategy to work your way to the top of the analytics pyramid. No matter which metrics you decide are best for you, ultimately your content marketing program should result in that "profitable customer action" mentioned in CMI's definition. Shares and Likes are great, but sales are the ultimate goal. The best content marketers have known this going back a century or more. The longevity of the discipline alone is a testament to the power of a well-executed content marketing strategy. In Chapter 2, let's see what content powerhouses from history—along with some more recent practitioners—have to teach us.

Chapter 2

The Best of 100+ Years of Content Marketing

Nothing is new under the sun. You've heard that old truism before, and it remains relevant in the case of content marketing. Long before blog posts and social media—or even television and the commercials that come along with it—companies realized the value of providing their customers with valuable information to create loyalty and drive action. As early as the 19th century, companies were implementing what we now recognize as content marketing, and what's even more remarkable is that today's companies are still using the same methods to get their messages to the masses.

There are a few examples that experts point to as the beginning of content marketing, and in many ways it is astounding how little has changed. In some cases, those grandfathers of the industry continue to use content marketing to inform, retain, and attract customers. More importantly, the techniques pioneered by these companies continue to be the foundation of content marketing across diverse brands and industries

From John Deere to Subaru

It's easy to think about content marketing as a technology-driven endeavor. Blogs and social media may have given content marketing a boost by lowering the barrier to entry, but content marketing has decidedly less high-tech roots (at least by our modern standards). It's commonly accepted that content marketing was born in 1895 to an Illinois blacksmith named John Deere. The founder of what would become one of the biggest farm machine supply companies in the world also started a magazine called *The Furrow* (see Figure 2.1).

Figure 2.1 A screenshot of *The Furrow,* one of the earliest examples of content marketing.

John Deere didn't set out to sell more tractors with *The Furrow.* The content was educational, teaching readers how to be more productive farmers, solving problems for the very people the company hoped to sell equipment to. Now, over a century later, Content Marketing Institute's (CMI) Joe Pulizzi calls *The Furrow* his favorite example of content marketing.

The Furrow is still going strong, only today the quarterly magazine has a companion website—and lots of imitators. Every few months Subaru sends me a magazine called *Drive* (see Figure 2.2). *Drive* is a lifestyle magazine for the "type" of consumers who drive Subarus, and it's the Japanese car maker's version of *The Furrow.* With *Drive* you never know what you might get. My favorite issue featured a cover story about the farm-to-table movement—I even confused it with an organic gardening magazine I also receive. It is both aspirational and relatable. Sometimes the content features tales of extreme athletes, and other times it's about archeologists (who just happen to be Forrester owners—which you only know because the vehicle appears in a picture of the archaeologist out in the field). Subaru does a nice job of intertwining content about topics it knows its brands owners are interested in with occasional, unobtrusive mentions of its own products. Perhaps the most interesting thing about this example is that the car company is targeting

Figure 2.2 Several examples of Subaru's *Drive* magazine.

existing customers, reminding them that the car company they trusted when they were climbing mountains will also be there when it's time to take the kids to the farmer's market.

A magazine filled with branded content is, perhaps, the oldest trick in the content marketing book—which is interesting considering the impact that the rise of content marketing has had on the bottom lines of so many publications (but that's a matter for a later chapter). Even CMI has its own magazine, *Chief Content Officer.* While the magazine might be a tried-and-true method of creating and disseminating content marketing, creating and printing a magazine may be out of the reach of most companies. Even creating a digital magazine might be a bigger commitment than some marketing departments can handle. No need to fear, there are plenty of other options.

From Jell-O to Whole Foods

Back in the 1880s, long before it was a household name, Jell-O was a small company looking to introduce its product to consumers. Imagine, please, what you might think if you were among the first people on earth to see a Jell-O mold and be told that you should incorporate this strange, new, gelatinous food into your family menu. You would, most likely, be wondering *What the heck am I supposed to do with this?* In 1904 Frank Woodward—who owned the rights to Jell-O—was desperate to figure out how to make this product turn a profit. Though he probably didn't have a name for it at the time, he turned to content marketing. Woodward started distributing free recipe books that, of course, incorporated Jell-O products. The rest is history.

This tactic is *de rigeur* today. Every box of macaroni and cheese or jar of salsa comes with recipe suggestions. Every company that sells food products—whether it's beans or caviar—lists its products' many uses on its website or, in the age of social media, on sites like Pinterest. And it isn't just the food producers that are in the content marketing game—the supermarkets are getting in on the action, too.

Right now, on my refrigerator, there is a flyer from Whole Foods Market explaining how I can make meals for four people for under $10. (This flyer is, no doubt, part of Whole Foods' strategy to dispel its "Whole Paycheck" image.) In my recipe box there are countless cards picked up from the aisles of Stew Leonard's and ShopRite. I don't even want to talk about how many pins on my "Yummies" board came from companies with a product to sell. The medium may have changed, but the general strategy behind the content has hardly changed at all.

Other Great Examples of Content Marketing

As I have already illustrated here, content marketing comes in a wide and wonderful variety of formats. While there are many high-profile examples—more of which we'll look at later in this chapter—some of the best examples are squirreled away on websites you may never have a reason to visit, or simply fly under the general public's radar. Here I would like to take a moment to look at a few of those.

The Lavin Agency

Most people will never have a reason to visit the Lavin Agency's site. The company represents a "select group of thinkers, writers, and doers for speaking engagements." Unless you happen to be

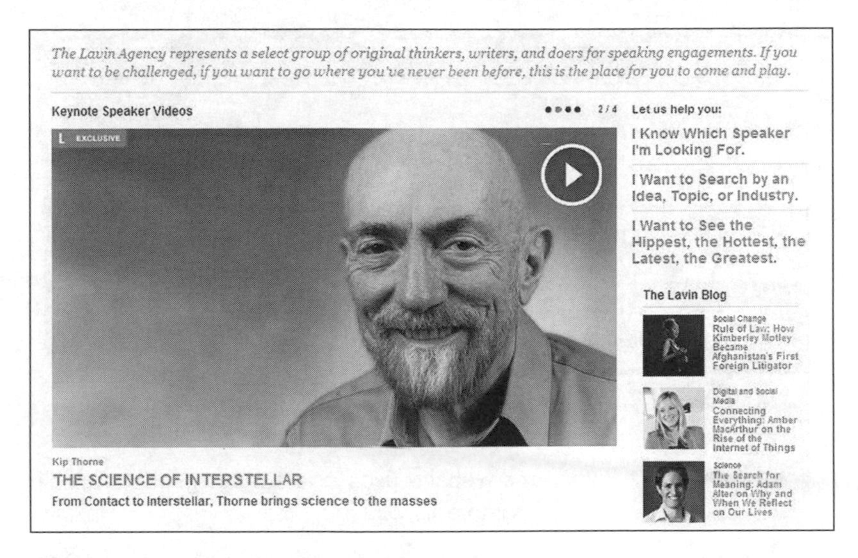

Figure 2.3 A screenshot from The Lavin Agency's website, which markets its roster of speakers through a series of informative videos.

trying to book one of its clients, you may never venture to the company's homepage, but that's a shame—especially if you're a fan of Ted Talks. As seen in Figure 2.3, the Lavin Agency hosts a number of videos that feature its speakers giving presentations on a wide-ranging group of topics—everything from why dangerous art is important to the rise of the Internet of Things. Those videos are also available on YouTube, because the agency knows people are far more likely to stumble upon its speaker videos there than they are if the videos are kept tucked away in its little corner of the web.

Petfinder

I'm willing to go out on a limb and assume that, unlike me, you don't spend hours combing through the listings for adoptable pets in your area on Petfinder.com (see Figure 2.4). But if you're in the market for a new rescue pet, Petfinder wants to be sure you come to its site to help make your decision. If you aren't in the market at the moment, Petfinder wants to be sure its site stays front and center in your mind so that, when the time comes, you use its services to find

Figure 2.4 Petfinder's website uses content marketing to promote its cause.

your next pet. And if you're on the fence, trying to decide whether a shelter pet is right for you, Petfinder wants to help you make your decision.

To accomplish these goals, Petfinder creates a variety of content that caters to everyone from people actively looking for a pet to people struggling with the issues so many pet owners face (i.e., behavioral and training challenges). But the goal here is a bit different than it is with many brands. Petfinder is not necessarily trying to sell you anything—though it certainly hopes you adopt one of the animals listed on its site—but instead sells advertisements. This is closer to a traditional publishing model, but it doesn't quite fit that mold either. After all, the goal is to help get homeless animals adopted (and selling advertising funds the content that fuels the objective), not just to create content for content's sake. (Content marketing confusion strikes again.)

Barbie on Instagram

I don't know about you, but I'm not willing to sit down and read a blog post about Barbie or any piece of inanimate plastic—though the idea of a blog "written" by Barbie could be sheer genius if done well. Much of Barbie's appeal is, of course, visual. There are Barbie movies out there, and while I'm sure people with children might

Figure 2.5 An example of the content found in Barbie's Instagram account.

be very familiar with them, many of us have never seen one (and hope we never will). So how does Barbie reach the rest of us? Instagram, duh! Yes, the doll has her own Instagram account (see Figure 2.5), with pictures of Barbie and her friends in fabulous clothes, gallivanting on the beach, and "at work." We get a glimpse of Barbie's super stylish apartment as well as videos of little girls playing with their dolls. Some of the photos look like *Vogue* photo shoots, and some are so cute and creative that even jaded folks like me have to smile. (That pumpkin patch photo really spoke to my New Englander's soul.)

Dollar Shave Club's Bathroom Minutes

Like a lot of people you may have a basket of reading material you keep in the bathroom. It's stuffed full of old magazines, catalogs, and maybe even a book. Well, Dollar Shave club knows how to take advantage of a captive audience when it sees one, and that's why all of its subscribers get a little pamphlet called "The Bathroom Minutes" with each shipment. Inside are puzzles, jokes, and anecdotes to keep you—and hopefully your guests—entertained during your extended stays in the bathroom. A lot of that same content can be found on the Dollar Shave Club blog (see Figure 2.6), where

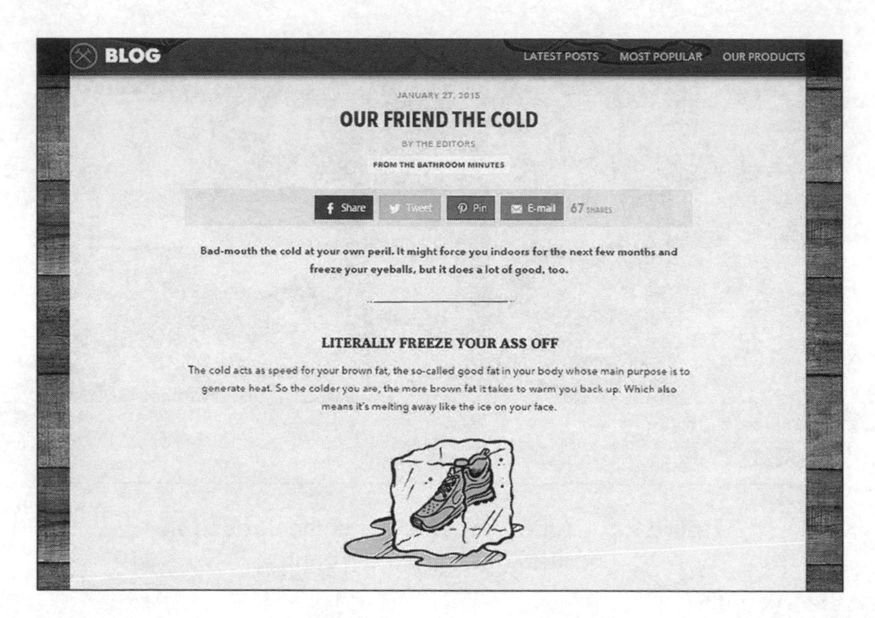

Figure 2.6 A screenshot of Dollar Shave Club's website, which uses its Bathroom Minutes to keep existing customers engaged.

anyone is free to read, and even more importantly, share. Maybe, after you're done solving the latest Rompecabeza (which loosely translates to "puzzle"), you'll order some razors—or add shaving cream to your existing order.

Red Bull: The Gold Standard

We're over 100 years in at this point, and for all we know cavemen were scribbling recipes on their walls to interest their fellow cavemen in their latest buffalo kill, but today, one company stands head and shoulders above the rest. Red Bull is so committed to its content marketing that it is often referred to as a media company that happens to sell an energy drink. In fact, it launched Red Bull Media House in 2007. According to a Contently case study by Erica Swallow, "[Red Bull] operates a TV station; prints one of the biggest magazines in the world; produces documentaries, movies and music; and runs a very thorough digital strategy..." There's even a Red Bull TV app on my smart TV, and I'd wager there is one on yours too (or your Roku, or PlayStation, or X-Box).

In September of 2014, Werner Brell, managing director of Red Bull Media House, made a rare public appearance at the Online Publisher Association's [now known as Digital Content Next] Content All Stars Event in New York to talk about the company's legendary content marketing—and I was lucky enough to be in attendance. "At Red Bull, our mission has always been to inspire and fascinate," Brell told the audience, and it does this through what he refers to as relevant content connected with an authentic brand.

Red Bull targeted athletes early on in its evolution by giving the energy drink away to skiers, windsurfers, and skateboarders. Brell said, "It's all about finding the right story for your brand and engaging the consumer in a way that he doesn't know he's being marketed to. Consumer engagement is the key...But none of this will work if you don't know your brand." It wouldn't be farfetched to say no company knows its brand—and its audience—better than Red Bull, and it has got the sales to back it up. At first, Brell said, people just bought the energy drink, but now brand loyalists buy movie tickets, watch television shows, buy event tickets, and more.

According to Brell, Red Bull had released 11 feature films over the previous three and a half years, including *Cerro Torre—A Snowball's Chance in Hell*. The movie chronicles David Lama's daring ascent of Cerro Torre, a notoriously dangerous mountain in Patagonia, and was released in European theaters in March of 2014. Red Bull Media House is also responsible for network shows like *All In with Laila Ali* on CBS, and countless other videos, magazines, and documentaries.

Red Bull's Rules for Great Content

1. Be relevant and authentic
2. Surprise and innovate
3. Be consistent
4. Be the story
5. Inspire sharing

Red Bull is so good at reaching a very specific—sometimes even niche—audience that much of its content goes unnoticed by those who aren't invested in extreme sports, but even the most casual Red Bull observer is probably familiar with one of the company's most famous content-related stunts. As Brian Morrissey put it best back in 2012 in "What Red Bull Can Teach Content Marketers" on Digiday: "The marketing world woke up today with Red Bull envy. At a time when brands talk of being publishers, Red Bull showed how this can be done on a grand scale: Enabling Felix Baumgartner to complete a historic (and awfully cool) skydive from 'the edge of space.'" You probably remember this stunt, even if you don't follow content marketing closely. (If you don't remember it, check out Figure 2.7 for a reminder.) The media couldn't stop talking about it, but this was just Red Bull's most high-profile attempt at getting your attention without actually "advertising." I mean, really, who can top flying a man to the edge of space and then letting him plummet to Earth while streaming it all on YouTube?

What makes Red Bull Stratos (the official name for the space jump) true content marketing and not just a crazy PR stunt—besides Red Bull's long-term commitment to content—is the well-executed

Figure 2.7 A screenshot from Felix Baumgartner's video of his Stratos jump sponsored by Red Bull.

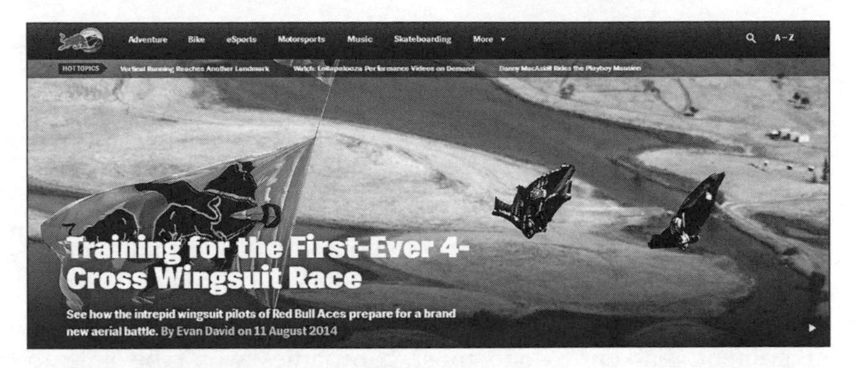

Figure 2.8 Red Bull's website puts content before product.

strategy that led to over 15 videos documenting the entire journey to the edge of space which resulted in hundreds of millions of views. Even when it isn't helping to launch men from the edge of earth's atmosphere, Red Bull is dedicated to content. A simple visit to its website (see Figure 2.8) will show you that it leads with content not products.

At times, it seems like Red Bull is only selling its energy drink to bankroll its media empire. (Not a bad idea. Publishers take note.) It's not true, though. Brell told the Content All Stars audience that each piece of content must have a revenue proposition attached. Sometimes that means there is a content sponsor, and other times it simply means selling ads or subscriptions to magazines. Whatever the case, Red Bull content has to earn its keep.

From a YouTube series chronicling the lives of extreme athletes to its own magazine, Red Bull creates a wide variety of content for an even wider variety of interests, but what can the average Joe take from this media juggernaut? Perhaps the greatest lesson is this: When you see a content vacuum, fill it. Red Bull saw that no one was catering to extreme sport enthusiasts and jumped in to fill the hole, and sold a whole lot of beverages in the meantime.

Branded Content at Its Best

If you took your kids to see *The LEGO Movie*—or just went to see it yourself—you may have realized (or not) that you were watching a giant commercial. Because the movie was so good, you—like most people—probably didn't care. Econsultancy asked the question, "*The LEGO Movie*: content marketing triumph or 100 minute advert?" For Robert Rose, it's the former. He says, "At the largest scale, *The LEGO Movie* is probably the most genius [content marketing] example I can think of at the moment." That statement would be hard to argue with, even if the movie hadn't brought in hundreds of millions of dollars at the box office and sold a ton of tie-in products. (That's ROI any marketer would envy.)

Making a feature-length Hollywood movie is an expensive piece of content marketing—one most companies won't be able to emulate—but Rose points to a couple more down-to-earth examples of excellent recent content marketing. For instance, GE's Six Second Science Fair experiments (#6SecondScience) encouraged users to submit videos of their home science experiments via Vine, the short video app (see Figure 2.9). The campaign has been an enormous success and relies mainly on free social media tools like Tumblr and Vine and user-generated content.

Even something as unsexy as welding can be made interesting through the power of good content. Rose says he really loves what Lincoln Electric—a provider of welding technology—did with its

Figure 2.9 A screenshot of General Electric's #6secondsciencefair challenge.

MadePossibleWith.com site where the company details its part in everything from the Grand Canyon skywalk to Indy car racing.

Content plays an especially important role for many born-digital businesses. Take Birchbox, for example. On its surface, Birchbox's business model—like Red Bull's—doesn't have much to do with content. For just $10 a month, the company sends subscribers a customized box filled with beauty supply samples and grooming goodies, helping customers save time and energy by delivering great products right to their doorsteps. Yet, the company employs an editorial director. It's Mollie Chen's job to recruit, engage, and retain customers using content, and she deploys a very specific strategy for Birchbox. As Mashable put it in "5 Businesses That Rock Content Marketing," "Birchbox's content marketing strategy targets the millennial generation's Achilles' heel: the fear of missing out (or FOMO, in internet slang)."

The content (see Figure 2.10) usually depicts happy customers and the great products they received in the most recent box to arrive in the mail, or gives everyone a peek at what's to come in the next delivery. As Stephanie Walden wrote in the Mashable article, "The message is simple: If you aren't getting Birchbox, you are definitely missing out—the perfect push to drive customers to whip out credit cards and subscribe."

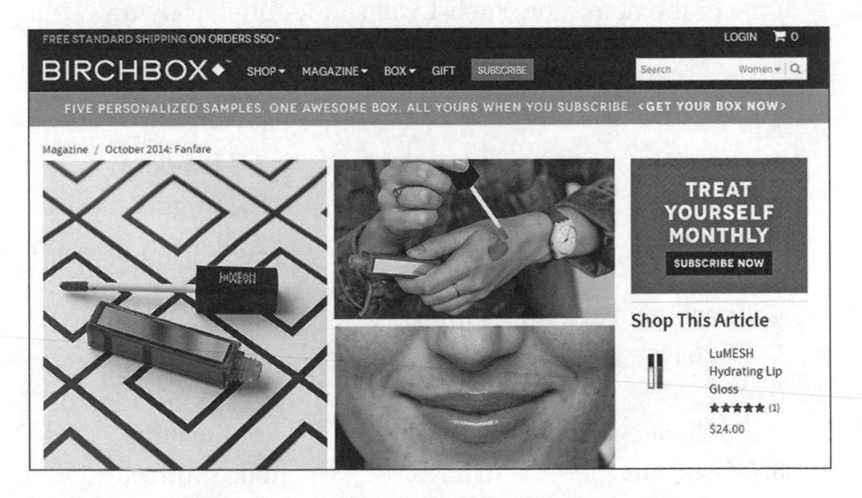

Figure 2.10 A screenshot of BirchBox's website. This firm puts content at the center of its marketing strategy.

Chen talked to MediaBistro about her role at Birchbox and the content marketing the company—founded by Chen and two friends—has become so famous for. It's almost deceptively simple. She said, "We approached it really simply: What would we, as women, want to read?" The content is perfectly crafted for Birchbox's huge social media following and has earned it a reputation as one of the best content marketers around—not to mention legions of devoted customers who gladly share pictures and videos of themselves enjoying the contents of their boxes. Birchbox brand advocates are so common on some social channels that it would be easy to mistake them for paid advertisers. But Birchbox knows that while brand advocates are great, it all means nothing if it doesn't amount to more sales. This is why every social media post the company shares links back to its own site, where a subscribe button is front and center.

Influential Content Marketing Brands

NewsCred—which provides content marketing software—published its list of "The Top 32 Most Influential Content Marketing Brands." Lauren Mangiaforte wrote, "So who's doing it really well? Which brands have rocked the boat and set the example? We scoured our archives and asked content marketers to weigh in, and here's our list of the 32 Top Content Marketing Brands of 2015."

Some of the names on the list will sound familiar by now, but others may surprise you.

NewsCred's Top 32

1. Denny's
2. General Electric
3. Lyft
4. Cheerios
5. Hello Flo
6. ALS
7. GoldieBlox
8. Maybelline
9. Taco Bell
10. Apple
11. AT&T
12. Coke
13. Refinery 29
14. Red Bull
15. Birchbox
16. Doritos
17. Whole Foods
18. Sharpie
19. GoPro
20. BHLDN
21. Home Depot
22. Nike
23. Gatorade
24. Pandora
25. Virgin America
26. Disney
27. KFC
28. Marriott
29. National Association of Realtors
30. Southwest Airlines
31. Barkbox
32. Panera Bread

Creating Your Own Classic Content

We all know the power of a great advertisement. Every winter we collectively sit around the television rapt by Super Bowl ads. Every last one of us knows what a Budweiser Clydesdale looks like. Some of us can still recall our favorite commercials from childhood. I was particularly fond of the "Where's the Beef?" lady. While most content marketing may not have quite the cultural reach of "Time to Make the Donuts"—with the exception of Red Bull's Stratos, which set the news shows abuzz—it's clear that if you get it right, your content marketing efforts can be effective far into the future.

EContent: *What tools do you recommend to everyone getting started in content marketing? Are there any new tools emerging to address the specific needs of content marketers that have impressed you?*

Joe Pulizzi: There are almost too many to mention. There are editorial and project management tools like DivvyHQ, Kapost, and AtTask. Marketing automation tools like Marketo, Oracle Eloqua, ActOn, Salesforce Pardot. Email marketing is more important than ever before. Analytics is critical. Social media management tools. I like LittleBird to help organize influencers.

Outside of this, I'm a big fan of LinkedIn's new publisher platform—it opened up the influencer program to all members.

But to be honest, the biggest issue for content marketing is that most marketers have no documented content marketing strategy. I would start the old-fashioned way and make sure you have a clear "why" for your business objective behind the program, a content marketing (editorial) mission statement, and an understanding of what it will take to build a sustained audience (like opt-in email subscribers).

Excerpted from "Q&A: Joe Pulizzi, Founder, Content Marketing Institute" (EContentmag.com)

Unfortunately, not every marketing department has Red Bull's budget—or its vision—but the wonderful thing about content marketing is that all that's really needed is a little imagination and the right people on your team. Fancy tools and means of distribution just aren't necessary. Anyone can set up a WordPress site and a few social media accounts in an afternoon. Free infographic creation tools abound. You don't need to be able to produce a monthly—or even quarterly—magazine, and you certainly don't need to help send a man to the edge of space. What you do need is the ability to tell a great story and respond to your audience's needs, no matter what form that takes. For some concrete ideas, refer to the step-by-step checklist to creating valuable content from Ahava Leibtag of Aha Media Group, reproduced in Figure 2.11.

What most of the examples I've laid out in this chapter have in common is that someone, somewhere along the way, thought outside the box. While *The Furrow* may not seem revolutionary now, there is no doubt that in his day John Deere was doing something unheard of. He provided a service and catered to the needs of his customers in a way no one had thought of before—and if you want to stand out in the age of information overload, you'll have to do the same.

Think about what LEGO did with its movie. Children's entertainment has a long history of spinning off toys, often making far more from its licensing and merchandising than it does from the shows or movies. Did you count all the Princess Elsas from Disney's *Frozen* that came to your door last Halloween? Have you peeked in a kid's toy box and counted the Transformers in there lately? But LEGO was, in many ways, at a disadvantage to some of its competitors in the toy market. LEGO had a long, storied history and, arguably, a superior product (after all, it's "never the same toy twice"), but it didn't have the promotional vehicles many toys for children do. So it decided to flip the script, so to speak, and instead of creating a toy based on a movie, LEGO made a movie based on a toy. (It's also worth mentioning that LEGO has a long history with content marketing, including a monthly magazine.)

Frankly, it's genius, but maybe not exactly something you can replicate. It is, however, an example you can learn from. It's never been easier to create and distribute video, but that also means you'll

CREATING VALUABLE CONTENT™

A Step-By-Step Checklist

IS THE CONTENT: / **DOES THE CONTENT INCLUDE:**

Findable

Can the user find the content?

- ☐ An h1 tag
- ☐ At least two h2 tags
- ☐ Metadata, including title, descriptors & keywords
- ☐ Links to other related content
- ☐ Alt tags for images

Readable

Can the user read the content?

- ☐ An inverted pyramid writing style
- ☐ Chunking
- ☐ Bullets
- ☐ Numbered lists
- ☐ Following the style guide

Understandable

Can the user understand the content?

- ☐ An appropriate content type (text, video, etc.)
- ☐ Reflection that you considered the user personas
- ☐ Context
- ☐ Respect for the audience's reading level
- ☐ Articulate and old idea in a new way

Actionable

Will the user want to take action?

- ☐ A call to action
- ☐ A place to comment
- ☐ An invitation to share
- ☐ Links to related content
- ☐ A direct summay of what to do

Shareable

Will the user share the content?

- ☐ Something to provoke an emotional response
- ☐ A reason to share
- ☐ An ask to share
- ☐ An easy way to share
- ☐ Personalization (add hashtags to tweets, etc.)

Figure 2.11 Aha Media Group's step-by-step checklist to creating valuable content.

have plenty of competition in that arena. So don't settle for mediocre content—LEGO didn't. It didn't try to compete on YouTube with countless (yet adorable) cat videos. LEGO didn't just greenlight a run-of-the-mill kids' movie that could have easily gone straight to DVD and been forgotten. It created something that delighted children and adults alike, and is destined to become a classic.

Every blog post you write isn't going to go down in history as one of the greats. Every video you make won't go viral. Luckily, they don't have to. What you need to do is to know how to reach your customers. LEGO's audience is, very likely, much bigger than yours. You don't need to be in multiplexes across the globe, but you do need—like any good marketer—to demonstrate that you know what your customers want, and give it to them. A well-crafted blog post that addresses a perennial problem can become a classic in its own right—solving dilemmas for years, or even decades, to come.

From Red Bull's media machine to LEGO's big budget blockbuster to GE's science shorts, content marketing wears dozens of different faces. Sometimes, it even looks easy to emulate—despite what the statistics tell us. While a lack of strategy and leadership is often to blame, there is one other problem: concentrating too much on marketing and not enough on content. But to strike the right balance needed to create classic content, you're going to need to hire the right people.

Chapter 3

Hire a Journalist as Your Chief Storyteller

If there's one thing I hope you've taken away from the first two chapters, it's that *creating great content ain't easy!* According to IMN's 2014 Content Marketing Survey, 42 percent of the content marketers surveyed said the primary challenge in implementing their strategies was "sourcing engaging content." Content Marketing Institute (CMI) research corroborates that finding. As seen in Figure 3.1, over 50 percent of B2B survey respondents in 2015 reported that producing engaging content is their biggest challenge.

Take a look a bit further down the list of complaints and you'll see that 34 percent of marketers think their internal teams are lacking skills and knowledge. The only thing surprising about this number is that it isn't higher. After all, how can you expect to create engaging content if you haven't hired the right people to do it? Developing truly great, useful content for your audience can be especially hard if you're used to being in marketing mode. Old habits die hard, which is why your marketing department needs a journalist. After all, there is a reason content marketing also goes by the name of brand journalism.

As far back as 2007, marketing guru David Meerman Scott was advocating for marketing departments to employ journalists. In 2010 he wrote on his WebInkNow blog, "I'm convinced that those with the traditional skills of marketing, public relations, advertising, and copywriting are not the right people to create brand journalism content. Instead you need the skills of a journalist."

In other words, you need a storyteller.

If the idea sounds crazy to you—which it might, if this is the first time you're hearing it—don't worry, there are plenty of companies already working with journalists that you can learn from. Among the companies heeding Scott's advice is Eloqua, a marketing

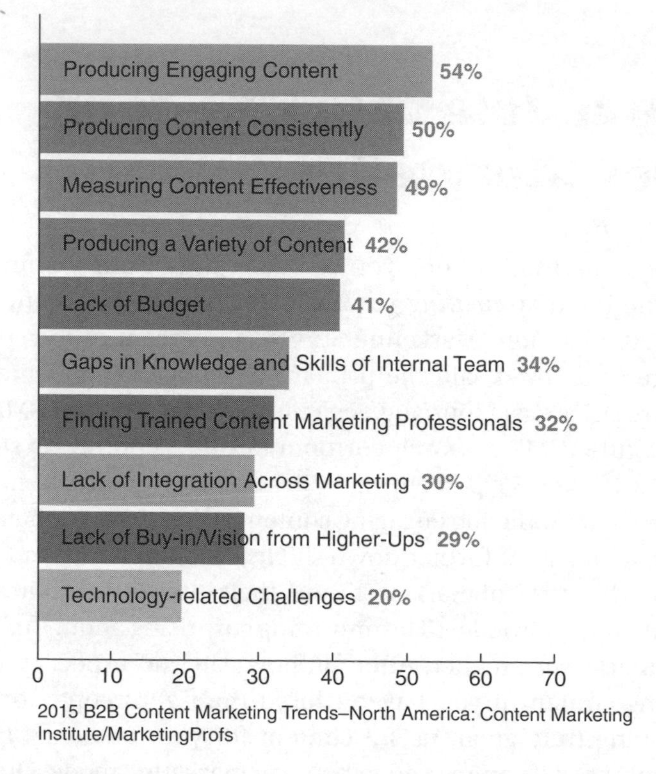

Figure 3.1 A chart from Content Marketing Institute reveals that producing engaging content is one of marketers' biggest challenges.

automation and cloud service, and it is even evangelizing about its decision. A blog post called "Hire a Journalist! (We did, and here's what we learned)" says, "Jesse is the real deal—a card-carrying journalist with credentials that include the *Boston Herald* and *Boston Business Journal.* One year ago, we hired Jesse and I want to celebrate by sharing with you what we've learned." (The post also credits David Meerman Scott with the idea to hire a reporter in the first place.)

From the sound of things, Eloqua had excellent results with its foray into brand journalism. According to the post, "The results have been fantastic, including thousands of new followers to our blog 'It's All About Revenue,' a Stevie Award for the blog, a doubling of unique visitors between Q2 and Q3 of this year, and thousands of new, valuable links. It has become the hub of our content marketing strategy."

This isn't a fly-by-night idea. Companies and journalists have already been teaming up for years with great success. But there are still some things you want to take into consideration.

Hiring the Right Journalist

Marketers may know what to look for when hiring a new social media manager or someone to write copy for commercials, but when looking for a storyteller, marketers may not know what qualities they need in a candidate. Evaluating a journalist's clips—especially one who has not been dabbling in content marketing—is an entirely different animal than judging a marketer's portfolio.

"Not all journalists make great content marketers—and not all great content marketers are journalists," says Robert Rose from CMI. "Knowing how to structure a story first, and then figure out the best way to tell it is the real difference. Marketers almost always start from medium first, then message to fill it. Great journalists go and get the *story* first, and then figure out the best way to tell it." This should be second nature to any good journalist, and it is key to the success of content marketing efforts.

Still, finding the right journalist for you is imperative to making your content marketing initiative thrive. As with any employee, it's important to find the right fit for your company's needs. Joe Pulizzi has some advice: "I'm not a big fan of 'generalist' journalists. I want someone who is deeply embedded into the industry. If I'm a brand, I'm stalking trade magazine mastheads looking for journalists that know, inside and out, what's going on in the industry. Those type of people can really take a brand's communication program to the next level."

If you don't know where to start looking for these insiders, one of the best ways to find specialized journalists is to turn to your Public Relations (PR) staff. For years your PR people have been hounding reporters and editors at trade magazines, as well as industry bloggers, to score that all-important earned media. They probably already have relationships with people they know and trust in the space, and can recommend a few candidates.

But not every brand needs a subject matter expert at the helm of its content marketing efforts. Red Bull isn't hiring beverage industry experts to create snowboarding videos or to interview Lenny Kravitz for *The Red Bulletin*—the aptly named print magazine.

A Checklist for Hiring Content Marketing Writers

Contributed by Jim Carberry

Writers are in high demand as companies start or expand content marketing teams. A Kapost survey of trends in content marketing hiring found nearly 45 percent of B2B companies plan to hire content marketing professionals. Writing and editing skills are the most important qualities companies seek in a content marketer, and writers are the first hired for teams.

While there's a broad and deep pool of writing talent on the market today, some companies are having difficulty hiring content marketers. Not every writer has the skills to create content that informs, engages and entertains audiences, champions a company's brand, generates and qualifies leads, promotes sales and builds customer loyalty.

Your next content marketing hire should have the following skills, abilities, and expertise, no matter what industry you're in.

- ☐ **Know business and marketing.** The writer needs to understand how the business world works and how businesses market their products and services. The writer knows not only how to create content but also how to market it.
- ☐ **Know your company.** Content writing isn't done in a vacuum. The writer knows your company's

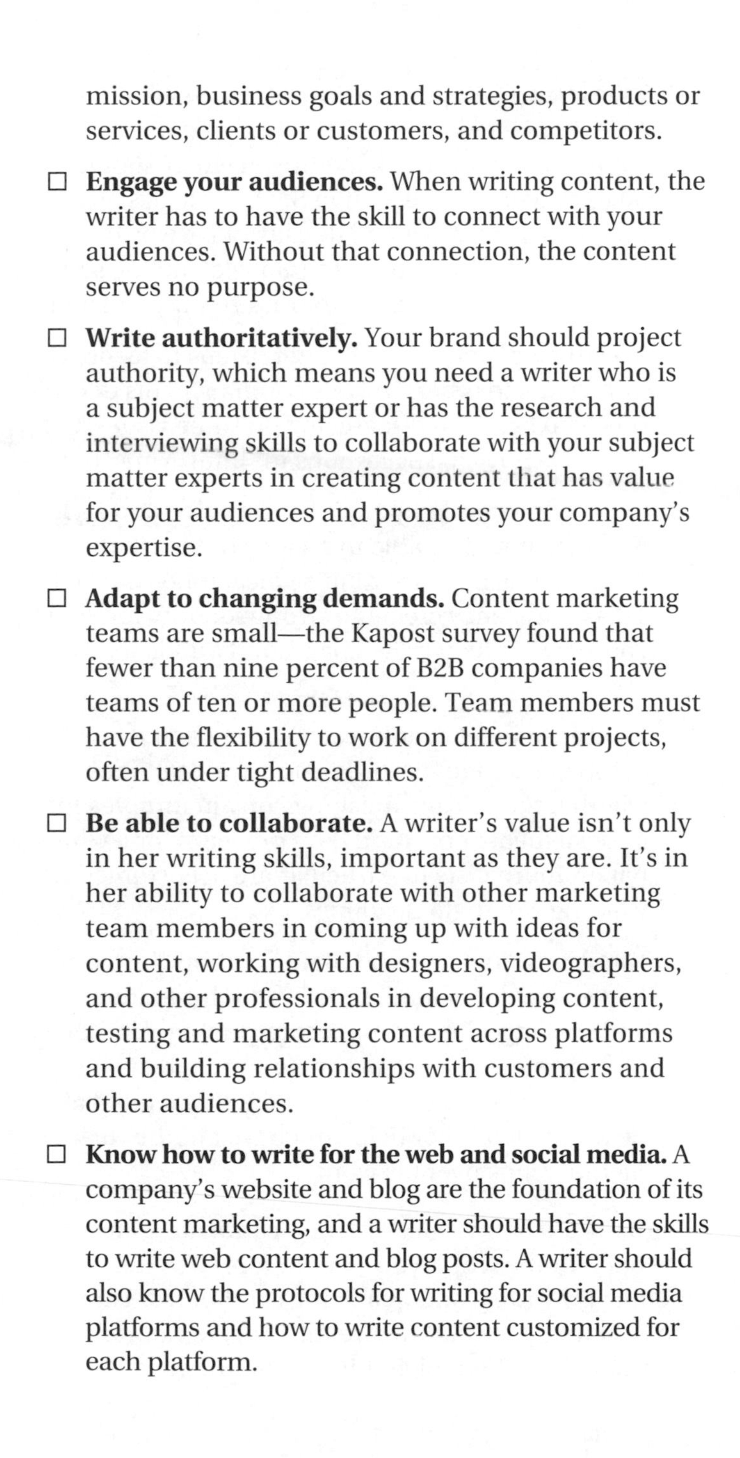

mission, business goals and strategies, products or services, clients or customers, and competitors.

- ☐ **Engage your audiences.** When writing content, the writer has to have the skill to connect with your audiences. Without that connection, the content serves no purpose.
- ☐ **Write authoritatively.** Your brand should project authority, which means you need a writer who is a subject matter expert or has the research and interviewing skills to collaborate with your subject matter experts in creating content that has value for your audiences and promotes your company's expertise.
- ☐ **Adapt to changing demands.** Content marketing teams are small—the Kapost survey found that fewer than nine percent of B2B companies have teams of ten or more people. Team members must have the flexibility to work on different projects, often under tight deadlines.
- ☐ **Be able to collaborate.** A writer's value isn't only in her writing skills, important as they are. It's in her ability to collaborate with other marketing team members in coming up with ideas for content, working with designers, videographers, and other professionals in developing content, testing and marketing content across platforms and building relationships with customers and other audiences.
- ☐ **Know how to write for the web and social media.** A company's website and blog are the foundation of its content marketing, and a writer should have the skills to write web content and blog posts. A writer should also know the protocols for writing for social media platforms and how to write content customized for each platform.

- ☐ **Know Search Engine Optimization (SEO).** As every marketer knows, SEO is fundamental to content creation and marketing. A writer should be thoroughly conversant in SEO: strategies, best practices, placement and density of keywords, testing methods, metrics, the Google ranking system, use of Google News alerts to track trends, and more.
- ☐ **Accept feedback.** A good writer listens to feedback from you and others in your company. This doesn't preclude her from disagreeing on some issues, but she's receptive to suggestions for improving content.
- ☐ **Adhere to your company's brand voice and style.** A writer should be able to create content that's consistent with your brand's voice, tone, and style. This consistency creates a strong identity for your company, enhances its image, and builds trust with audiences.
- ☐ **Be able to meet deadlines.** A writer should complete content according to your deadlines, whether that means finishing copy in minutes for a social media post or in days or weeks for a white paper. Journalists in particular are accustomed to working with tight deadlines.
- ☐ **Know how to proofread.** Before submitting copy to you, a writer should proofread it for grammar and spelling, check it for accuracy in names, dates, places, references, facts and figures, and ensure that it is correctly formatted. But the writer should also be willing to ask for help, and have another team member look over his work.

With the aid of this checklist, you can write a job description of the writer you want to hire. Use it in searching for writers and qualifying candidates. Think about whether you want to hire full time, temporary, or freelance writers. You might hire a full time writer, one who could learn your company inside and out and write content for all of your company's platforms. That writer could assist you in hiring freelance writers for special projects; for example, a writer skilled and experienced in writing presentations might work with your CEO in creating a presentation to the company's shareholders.

Once you know exactly what skills and traits you need, you can find the content marketing writer you want in a sea of talent. The search takes time, patience, and effort, but you'll be rewarded with content that stands out from the competition, promotes your brand, engages audiences, and attracts loyal customers.

Jim Carberry is a former Wall Street Journal *reporter who provides writing and editing services to business clients.*

Easing the Transition

As valuable as a journalist can be to your content marketing efforts, you may need to allow some time for acclimation. Your journalist will, no doubt, be used to the fast-paced atmosphere of a newsroom, where story ideas come in through the constant barrage of emails from PR people. Chances are your journalist—who probably came from a publication with a constant need for more content—will also be used to working at a much faster pace than you demand (but that can be a good thing, especially if you're struggling to create enough content). Learning to adjust to a different way of doing things may be difficult. Meanwhile, your marketers may have trouble understanding that journalists are not there to *sell, sell, sell!*

The Eloqua post has some sage advice for making sure your new brand journalist is a success—including how to integrate them into your team and teach them complementary skills—but perhaps the most important piece of advice is this: "Give the journalist room to breathe, and for goodness sake, don't ask the reporter to shill."

Remember, you hired this person for a reason. She knows how to create compelling content that will set your company apart as a thought-leader. Don't make the mistake of imposing your old marketing ways on her, because you won't get the results you're looking for—and neither of you will be happy.

Education is also important. I'll go into this in more depth in the next section of the book, but it's still important to note here that while journalists may be natural storytellers, they may need some help getting up to speed on the marketing side of the equation—as well as with the technology. If you're looking to create multimedia content, you may need your journalists to take a refresher course on video or audio editing (depending on their skills, of course). Rest assured, it's a lot easier to teach a journalist to look at a story with a marketer's eye than it is to teach a marketer to stop selling and start storytelling!

The Myth of the Shrinking Attention Span (or Why You Need a Storyteller)

I've been thinking a lot about attention span lately. Since the advent of Twitter, we've been told that the our audience is no longer capable of maintaining interest in what we have to say if it's more than 140 characters long. Then Vine appeared on the scene with 6-second videos, and panic nearly ensued. Meanwhile, though, millions of Americans sat down on their couches to binge watch entire seasons of *Orange Is the New Black*. Clearly, the public-at-large is perfectly capable of paying attention when they want to. So what are we to conclude from this information? The problem isn't your audience's attention span—it's your content.

It's hard to make a case for the shrinking attention span when people are spending entire weekends in front of their television (or whatever screen they're watching programming on), wondering what Francis Underwood is going to do next on *House of Cards*. But let's move away from the world of addictive Netflix originals for a moment and talk about podcasts. That business is booming, and there is no clearer indication that people want great, long-form content.

Podcast networks are popping up like dandelions in your lawn—only no one is likely to come along and weed out these networks. American Public Media has "Infinite Guest," while Public Radio International (PRI) has "SoundWorks," and Public Radio Exchange (PRX) has "Radiotopia." And if we want to get really meta about it, former *This American Life* producer, Alex Blumberg, left the show to start his own podcast company, and he's podcasting about the experience.

Speaking of *This American Life*, the popular radio show spurred its own podcast offshoot called "Serial." "Serial" took the podcasting world—and pop culture—by storm. The show follows one story each season—in the case of Season One, a 15-year-old murder—looking at each aspect in-depth. Throughout the premiere season, millions of listeners, myself included, were left pacing and nervously scratching like addicts, waiting to find out what would happen next. And when it was over, we couldn't wait for the second season—which leads to podcasts about the podcasts rocketing up the iTunes charts.

This is ultra-long-form storytelling. "Serial" stretches out one story during an entire season—almost like *The Wire* of podcasts. It not only asks listeners to take the time to listen but to wait an entire week to find out what happens next. In the TV world, this is nothing new, but for podcasts, this is darn near revolutionary.

The spinoff, hosted by *This American Life's* Sarah Koenig, is taking advantage of one of the main benefits of podcasting, which is that each episode can be as long or short as it needs to be. Some episodes are an hour long, while others barely scratch the half-hour mark. That's the beauty of podcasting though, right? You can pretty much do whatever you want—or need—to do.

Longform.org also knows that there is still an audience for in-depth, relevant content, which is why it curates the best in long-form journalism and makes it accessible and easy to find via its site. Still, the myth of the shrinking attention span persists. A quick Google search will turn up plenty of advice on how to market to people with shrinking attention spans. So why does this idea about people who just can't concentrate on anything continue to plague us?

Blame the attention economy. We all jump around on the internet, I won't dispute that. We're inundated and constantly looking for the piece of content that is actually going to grab our attention and make us finish it. Attention is a finite resource but content is seemingly infinite,so like my hard earned cash, you better make your content worth my time. This is why storytelling is so important. You can tick off statistics and bore your audience to no end—causing them to click to the next page—or you can tell them a story that compels them to read, listen, or watch until the end.

Of course, there are times when brevity works in your favor. On mobile devices, for instance, context is everything. Few people want to read a 3,000-word piece on a tiny screen (and those screens are getting tinier as wearables increasingly come into play). Breaking news also lends itself well to short formats, especially when you're competing against hundreds of other outlets for eyeballs. Your time and resources are better spent on creating content that can help you stand out from the crowd—provide analysis or entertain in a way no one else can. So if your audience isn't finishing your two-minute video or your 500-word blog post, don't blame anyone but yourself.

When in Doubt, Hire a Freelancer

Perhaps you're interested in working with a journalist but aren't quite ready to make the move and hire one full-time. Lucky for you there's a solution to that problem: freelancers.

It is estimated that by 2020 freelancers and temps will make up nearly 20 percent of the workforce. As newsrooms close down, and the freelance economy grows, there will be more and more journalists looking to create content for brands. Working with one of these professionals is a great solution for companies without the budget for a full-time brand journalist, or one that just isn't ready to take the plunge. (Heck, you might even end up trying to hire that person later!)

But finding the right fit with a freelancer is just as important as if you were hiring that person full-time—at least for your content, if not for your HR department. Again, you can turn to your PR folks who have contacts in the journalism space; there are also plenty of services popping up with the aim of connecting companies and content creators. There are general services like Freelancer.com, but Contently has emerged over the past few years as a destination for companies and freelancers focused on content marketing to find one another.

Contently was cofounded by journalist Shane Snow—who now also serves as the company's chief creative officer—in part because Snow understood, more than anyone, how tough freelancing can be. He says, "When I graduated from journalism school, I entered the job market as a freelancer. So did most of my classmates, I noticed. Getting a master's degree at a top journalism school only to have to strike out on your own was tough to swallow on multiple levels. With freelancing came a host of things that have nothing to do with the craft, I observed: finding work, hassling clients to pay you, marketing yourself, getting found in Google, doing self-employment taxes, and so on."

Of course, the difficult life of a full-time freelancer is nothing new. In fact, it's a problem a number of companies have been trying to solve for years. But Snow noticed something new in the atmosphere: "At the same time, a friend of mine was looking to hire trained journalists to blog for his business. He and I talked and realized that there was an untapped opportunity to match trained, professional journalists with freelance work online, and we soon realized that some of the well-paying gigs were going to be from brands doing content marketing."

A shift had occurred. Sure, freelancers were still pitching their story ideas to editors at newspapers, magazines, and websites, but the real money was in content marketing. Now all they had to do was find the marketing departments in need.

"We thought that by providing an ecosystem where the two parties could work together—and by taking care of the administrative stuff ourselves—we could provide enough value to make both freelancers' and businesses' jobs easier," says Snow. "We were also excited by the chance to support the future of journalism while putting better content online, so we focused on only high-paying, high-quality gigs, and started our own foundation for investigative journalism using our profits."

Snow echoes the advice of Joe Pulizzi and Eloqua when it comes to finding the right journalist for your team and making the transition easy on everyone. "It's important to be ethical, and make sure you never ask a journalist to do something they'd be uncomfortable with. Sometimes brands aren't clear on what that might be," Snow says. He recommends heading to contently.com/ethics to get an idea of your boundaries as a brand. He continues, "When hiring journalists, you want good subject matter expertise and/or a personality who has built a following on a particular topic. That's more powerful than hiring a generalist (unless you are looking for them to cover a breadth of topics, in which case the opposite is true). This is where Contently comes in, we use data about writers' past work to make it easy for brands to connect with the right fit."

What It's Like to Work With Contently

Haniya Rae is a freelancer who has a not-so-typical relationship with Contently. She was working as an assistant editor at Digiday, covering marketing and advertising, when a Contently editor contacted her, wanting to know if Rae would be interested in writing for its sites The Freelancer or The Content Strategist. Unfortunately Rae had a noncompete clause, but the offer got her thinking and by the time I talked with her, she had been a full-time freelancer for about seven months.

Rae got started on her new career path by writing for Contently, but it wasn't long before she was being matched with brands just like the other writers using the platform. Typically, Rae says, an account manager from Contently will contact her on behalf of a

Do You Need an Agency?

Sometimes handling your content marketing in-house is just not an option. That's where agencies come in. Your marketing agency may have some employees focused on content marketing, but there are also specialized content marketing agencies that can help you with your content needs. In "How to Know When You Need a Content Marketing Agency" on CMI's website, Kathryn Hawkins describes a few scenarios where hiring a specialized agency may be in your best interest:

- Early-stage startups that need a flexible marketing solution
- Mid-sized or large organizations without sufficient internal resources
- Organizations with temporary staffing challenges
- Business professionals who want to build their industry reputation
- Marketing agencies without in-house content marketing expertise

This is a pretty broad ranging list, but here's what I take away from it: If you don't have in-house expertise—and I do mean *expertise*, not just experience (or a vague idea of how to create content)—it's important to seek it out. I would argue that you should be hiring someone, but if that's not possible, an agency is a viable alternative.

brand. That content-matchmaker has already assessed the client's needs and taken a look at Rae's Contently portfolio and decided that she is a good match. Once she accepts the job, Contently helps keep her on track with a calendar of deadlines. Rae eventually turns in her work via a content management system that she says is akin to a high-end word processor. This is where one of the main selling points comes in. As soon as she turns in her work, Contently pays her via PayPal. Every freelancer knows that, other than finding work, getting paid is one of the toughest aspects of freelancing, but Contently makes both of those processes run a bit more smoothly.

In her first six months as a freelancer, Rae estimates Contently had paired her with four different clients. Some of those jobs were one-time projects while others were more regular gigs—like monthly blog posts. In general, she says it's been a good experience, although there are some kinks still being worked out. Rae says that one problem that can come up is the scope of work expected for a project. Because there isn't a contract between the writer and the company, she says that sometimes the client can have unreasonable expectations for revisions for no extra money. She does say, however, that Contently is always good about backing up their writers while also trying to keep the client happy. Because all communication is supposed to take place through the Contently platform, account managers have access to conversations between freelancers and brands and can help mediate any disputes.

Like many freelancers, Rae splits her time between content marketing gigs and more traditional journalism. This could easily raise some ethical red flags, but she has an easy way of dealing with those concerns. When it comes to branded content, she sticks with covering advertising and marketing. This allows her to branch out and cover her passions of design and architecture in more traditional journalism settings.

Keeping these two worlds separate has worked well for Rae, but she does know freelancers who have had their worlds collide. One friend who covers real estate has been asked to create content for a real estate company and had to turn the job down. This—as you may have already noticed—makes it a bit harder for brands to follow the advice of the experts and hire journalists from your industry, at least on a freelance basis. Many content creators, like Rae, have managed to find a balance that works for everyone involved.

Even with her own "Chinese Wall" set up to keep her content marketing jobs separated from her journalistic persona, Rae still manages to book some content marketing gigs that are exciting and challenging. For instance, she points to a job writing articles for *AdWeek's* marketing arm which produces a physical book—or hefty magazine—for Advertising Week.

Contently may not be the answer for every marketing department looking for content creators, but if 50 percent of marketers are struggling to keep up with content demands and 34 percent think their internal teams are lacking in content marketing skills, then they are going to have to find new talent somewhere. Rae says that when she first began freelancing, Contently clients made up about 50 percent of her business, but as she's built a reputation and word of mouth has spread, she's relied less on the service. Now she estimates that 20–30 percent of her work comes through the platform. Brands could take a lesson from her and look to Contently as a bridge, using the service and its account managers to help them find talent—and learn exactly what to look for in a new hire without making a major commitment.

Curate Your Way to More Content

Content marketing isn't all about content creation—sometimes it's about curation. If your team is having trouble keeping up with the content demands of your audience—even after you've hired a team of star journalists—then it's time to turn to other content creators for help.

"Brands are looking to become the primary destination of insights and information on the topics that matter to their customers. Curation is really important to achieving that goal," says Michael Brenner, head of strategy at NewsCred. "While brands are building effective content creation approaches, they are also learning that you can't cover every topic, from every angle. So curation is an effective mechanism for covering the stories that matter to your audience, often by licensing images from the best photographers in the world or articles from the best publishers in the world."

Curation can help you flesh out your content efforts, but if you do it wrong you can damage your brand. The content you share with your audience needs to be high quality, whether you create it or not. Anthony Gaenzle wrote in "How to Increase Content Curation without Hiring More People" for CMI, "There are different

What Is Content Curation?

"Content Curation is the act of discovering, gathering, and presenting digital content that surrounds specific subject matter. Though it is still considered a 'buzz word' by many in the content world, content curation is now becoming a marketing staple for many companies with a successful online presence.

"Unlike content marketing, content curation does not include generating content, but instead, amassing content from a variety of sources, and delivering it in an organized fashion. For instance, a content curator is not necessarily responsible for creating new content, but instead, for finding relevant content pertaining to a specific category and funneling this information to readers in a mash-up style."

Eileen Mullan, EContentmag.com

schools of thought on content curation, and I urge you to approach this one with care, but there is certainly value in it if done properly. I am not recommending that you simply post the first paragraph or two with a link to the original article. I don't see a lot of value in that."

Gaenzle reminds us that Google does not reward SEO efforts for those kinds of posts, and you'll likely just lose the traffic to the third party anyway. He does, however, have a couple of suggestions for how to make this kind of curation work for you. Basically, he suggests taking the most important part of the article and putting it at the heart of your post and bookending it with your own content—an introduction and a conclusion that adds some kind of value. You may also want to link to your own content to get readers deeper into your site. If you spend any amount of time on the web, it's likely that you see exactly this kind of content all the time.

But if you want to get a bit more sophisticated with your curation efforts, Brenner has some advice. "Brands new to content marketing should be seeking to become the best source of information on the topics that relate to their business. To do so, they must do content curation really well," says Brenner. "I have two main tips. First, brands have to cover the top stories 'like a journalist' would and that means thinking and acting like a publisher. When you do this, you begin to see other publishers as great sources of the information you can provide your audience. Second, you have to provide what I call 'the best answer on the internet' and often that means borrowing on the authority of other sources. Content curation and licensing allows you to do that."

Of course, NewsCred would like to help you with that curation and licensing—and maybe help some publishers get exposure for their content in the meantime. "NewsCred is helping brands find content that is relevant and fitting for their campaigns at scale," says Jennifer Stenger, director of publisher development at NewsCred. "We are simultaneously giving the publisher's content a new shelf life. We discover and package content around very specific topics, which sometimes includes older articles. We find this content new value and a secondary revenue stream for the publisher for content they've already produced, already maximized on their own site and directly monetized."

"Brands want to use the NewsCred platform because it gives them access to everything they need in one place," says Stenger. "They do not wish to enter into multiple licensing agreements, get access to content in many different ways and have to sift through to find the needles in the haystacks of articles."

"Convince and Convert" Takes on New Meaning

Hopefully it now seems like a no-brainer for your marketing team to hire a journalist as your chief storyteller. Now you just have to find and convince the right content creator(s) to jump on the branded content bandwagon. That may prove to be the hardest step on your content marketing journey.

The best journalists may be hard to convert to content marketers. Many may still be dreaming of winning a Pulitzer or breaking the next big political scandal. Selling soap, soda, or whatever it is your company is making may not be the career path they had in mind. But don't worry, I will help you make your case in Part II.

Part II

A New Road for Journalists

Chapter 4

The Changing Face of Journalism

Newsrooms don't look like they used to. Budgets are shrinking and so are staff numbers. The rise of digital media, the 24-hour news cycle, and declining ad revenue are forcing newspapers and magazines to completely reimagine their business models. Meanwhile, reporters have to contend with citizen journalists on social media. Many cub reporters coming out of journalism school can't find full-time jobs and have to cobble together a living from freelance gigs. As dire as the news may sound, plenty of opportunity is opening up outside of the newsrooms at big media outlets—and in many ways, it has helped move journalism forward while also forcing aspiring writers to get creative and seek new paths.

Alternative sources for news with novel monetization models have started popping up all across the internet. According to Richard Pérez-Peña's article "As Shrinking Newsrooms Use Upstarts' Content, Vetting Questions Arise" in the *New York Times*, "With established newsrooms shrinking, a raft of smaller news outlets have cropped up in the last few years, selling or simply giving news reports to the traditional media—groups like ProPublica, Global Post, Politico and Kaiser Health News." Many journalists are finding jobs at just these kinds of upstarts. Many more find jobs at digital-only publications like Huffington Post or the Gawker Media sites—or the ever popular and constantly transforming Buzzfeed."

These media startups are doing everything from in-depth, long-form journalism to breezy, blog-style posts. Some of them are raking in cash while others are winning journalism's most prestigious prizes. In 2013, *EContent* columnist Ron Miller wrote about a plucky publication named InsideClimate News. With a staff of just seven people and no actual office, it won the Pulitzer Prize for "The Dilbit Disaster: Inside the Biggest Oil Spill You've Never Heard Of." He wrote: "This small company was able to outmaneuver the big boys, because it pays attention to just one area: the climate. It's worth noting that the *New York Times* closed its environmental desk earlier this year. Because large news organizations are letting news like this slip, the smaller organization with a laser-focus is able to fill the gap…What InsideClimate News has shown more than anything, though, is that a small group of committed individuals can find ways to tell stories that truly matter without a ton of money? And that has always been the story of the internet. It has broken down barriers and given people with an idea the means to see it through without a ton of financial backing. And it might be that this little company could embody the future of investigative journalism: small, lean, and totally focused."

The news for journalism as a practice may not be as bleak as some have predicted, but smaller, digital newsrooms mean fewer jobs for journalists, period. Ken Doctor wrote in a post on Newsonomics.com, "We talk about the economics of print vs. online vs. hybrid, and I've guesstimated that if metro dailies indeed flipped the switch [to digital-only distribution], they'd be able to 'afford' about 15% of their newsroom staffs."

That is a sobering number. Digital start-ups may be able to pick up some of the slack, but it's highly unlikely the world will ever need as many journalists as it once demanded. That being said, the demand for content has never been higher. If journalists are able to embrace the changing industry, and see past old prejudices about working outside the newsroom, new and exciting opportunities will abound.

Banner Blindness and the Rise of Native Advertising

The myriad factors contributing to the struggles of traditional print media are too numerous to name and not necessarily germane to our mission here, but one problem plaguing sales reps tasked with selling online advertising is something known as banner blindness—and, to some degree, content marketing has been the answer.

According to BannerBlindness.org, this phenomena is nothing new. In fact it goes back as far as dial-up modems, AOL accounts, and Netscape. The organization's About page has this to say: "The term 'banner blindness' was coined in 1997 when Jakob Nielson published a study describing his findings on the matter for the first time. Using eye tracking heat maps, the web usability guru was able to view what his participants' eyes focused on or where they fluttered to on a given website, in order to discover if website visitors looked at banner advertisements. Nielson revealed that not only did his participants avoid looking in the general direction of ads, but they also avoided looking in an area they presumed ads to be placed."

In many ways, digital ads would seem to stand head and shoulders above print ads in terms of effectiveness. Now, in the age of analytics, a website can pinpoint exactly who is viewing its content, on what device, and serve up personalized ads. In turn, they can tell advertisers far more about who saw and clicked on their ads than ever before. Unfortunately, that audience is mostly ignoring the traditional banner ads that have long been the staple of the digital media. And thanks to unlimited inventory, online ads have never commanded the same price as their print counterparts. This double-whammy has served to shape the future of publishers' monetization models.

Among the solutions that have evolved to solve publishers' revenue problems is the often controversial native advertising. Jakob Nielson understood way back in 1997 that this type of solution may be necessary. According to BannerBlindness.org, "Nielson was reluctant to admit that one of the answers to banner blindness was to trick the reader into thinking an advertisement was not what it appeared to be. In other words, make an ad look less like an ad by altering its appearance and placement." That is a pretty good description of what native advertising has become.

Not all native advertising is content marketing, or vice versa, but there is often significant overlap between the two. Without this new source of income, many media companies—both print and digital—may not have survived. According to the Online Publishers Association (now Digital Content Next) study, "Premium Content Brands Are Native Naturals," "73 percent of OPA members surveyed currently offer native advertising solutions, with the potential to reach 90 percent by the end of 2013." Several years on, it's safe to say that native advertising has reached full capacity among the group's members, and with that comes a whole new set of jobs for journalists.

What Is Native Advertising?

Advertisers have long struggled to truly engage audiences. For many years, the web seemed like it might solve that problem, until advertisers realized potential customers ignored banner ads just as they skip past commercials on the DVR. But that didn't stop advertisers from trying to use the Enter: Native Advertising.

Often confused with content marketing and advertorials, native advertising is different than either of these other tactics. As Michael Raybman put it on iMedia, "In my view, it is defined as content that seamlessly blends into the context, design, and functionality of every page that it appears on, while being overt about its sales intention." Wikipedia adds, "The advertiser's intent is to make the paid advertising feel less intrusive and thus increase the likelihood users will click on it."

Native advertising, however, changes from one context to the next appearing in every possible format: video, images, articles, etc. The shape-shifting nature of this form of advertising makes it hard to spot—and explains why it is so often confused/overlaps with other popular types of advertising. The integrated nature of the ads also makes some people uncomfortable as they often blur the lines between editorial and advertising content.

EContentmag.com

The Breakdown of Church and State

The media isn't governed by a constitution that promises a separation between church and state—otherwise known as editorial and marketing. Nonetheless, we've come to expect a certain voluntary regulation from our news providers that makes sure journalists and editors aren't worried about commercial concerns as they cover the news. As branded content makes its way deeper into the publishing landscape, the so called Chinese Wall that has protected journalists from their colleagues in the sales department is crumbling. The blurring of the lines between editorial and marketing has many people worried, but there is no denying that without branded content and native advertising, the forecast for digital media would be bleak.

However, you don't have to look far to realize that our expectation of unbiased news coverage is relatively new. Ira Basen wrote an article titled "Breaking Down the Wall" for the University of Wisconsin's Center for Journalism Ethics, where he detailed the changes the profession has under gone throughout the decades: "Once upon a time, running a newspaper was a fairly simple proposition...I'm talking about a period that began in the U.S. in colonial times and ended in the early decades of the 19th century. It was a time when newspapers were essentially house organs of political parties or commercial interests, when editors and publishers knew which side their bread was buttered on, and there was no need to spend a lot of time agonizing over what stories needed to be covered and how and where they would appear in the paper."

In many corners of journalism this is still the reality—and I'm not just talking about state-owned media in countries like Russia or North Korea. Turn on your television and flip over to FOX News and any remaining illusions you might have about the unbiased nature of journalism will be quickly shattered. Of course, FOX News devotees might dismiss MSNBC, the *New York Times,* or even NPR as nothing but liberal propaganda. Documents revealed in the Sony hacking scandal revealed that even the celebrity puff pieces are less than "fair and balanced." In one case, reported by Gawker, the chairman of TriStar—a Sony division—quibbled over the use of "some" instead of "many" in an article, and the public relations staff was able to get other stories canceled. In fact, Sony was able to keep us all from hearing about *Ishtar*—the legendary flop—finally becoming a moneymaker after a couple of decades (see Figure 4.1). For shame!

While our media may not be quite as independent as we like to believe, the state of the media seems to have, generally, improved since the days when the newspapers were bought and paid for by business and political interests. Basen wrote that advertising is

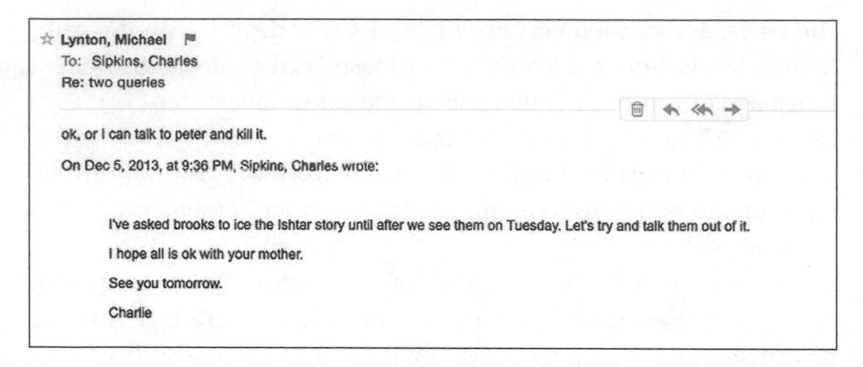
Lynton, Michael
To: Sipkins, Charles
Re: two queries

ok, or I can talk to peter and kill it.

On Dec 5, 2013, at 9:36 PM, Sipkins, Charles wrote:

I've asked brooks to ice the Ishtar story until after we see them on Tuesday. Let's try and talk them out of it.

I hope all is ok with your mother.

See you tomorrow.

Charlie

Figure 4.1 This email from the Sony leak helped prove that media isn't always as independent as we would like to think.

what changed all of that. Publishers saw the potential of a bigger pay day, and things started to change. According to Basen, "In 1870, only 13 percent of daily newspapers in the 50 biggest U.S. cities identified themselves as 'independent.' By 1900, 47 percent of them did. By then, advertising revenue made up 55 percent of total newspaper revenue." Our modern idea of journalism began to take shape, but even then, something like native advertising was floating around. Basen wrote, "The typical North American newspaper at the turn of the century would frequently feature three types of content on the page: news, advertising, and a hybrid that was essentially advertising disguised to look like news."

Unlike today's native advertising, there were no disclaimers or warnings that the content was sponsored. By the 1920s, though, that "Chinese Wall" was starting to go up, and the practice of hiding ads in the editorial content was being frowned on. And until recently, newspapers at least tried to operate with a split down the middle of their organizations that kept reporters out of the concerns of the business department and vice versa. Basen is more than a little critical of custom content, and there are certainly plenty of publishers that still haven't managed to strike the right balance, but that doesn't mean there isn't an ethical way to create a branded content strategy.

My point here is not to make the case for or against native advertising but to make it clear that the media industry is changing rapidly. Journalists are realizing that between the shrinking newsrooms and that diminishing divide between editorial and marketing content, those jobs they dreamed about in J-school are few and far between. Just like the newspapers they had hoped to work for, writers are getting creative to build a career that is fulfilling and ethical. Whether you go to work for a brand, an agency, or for one of the "content studios" popping up at newspapers and magazines, the new opportunities for great storytellers are endless.

EContent: *Content marketing and native advertising are often talked about in the same breath. How do you differentiate between the two when talking with critics of native advertising?*

Joe Pulizzi: Native advertising is part of the content marketing approach, but only slightly. The content marketing approach is our strategy behind creating behavior change with customers and prospects by creating and distributing valuable and consistent information (read: non-sales). Native advertising is leveraging part of that strategy on someone else's platform, while paying to do it. That's where native gets a little blurry. It's clearly advertising because it's paid, but it generally is educational or entertaining in nature so that people will actually pay attention to it.

If you are a brand, your job is to steal attention from the publisher's platform and make it your own. As a publisher, you are giving away a piece of your credibility and platform to your advertisers, which can be a risky proposition for some.

All that said, brands can execute a content marketing strategy without leveraging native at all, and some brands can engage in native advertising without really creating a sustained content program.

Excerpted from "Q&A: Joe Pulizzi, Founder, Content Marketing Institute" (EContentmag.com)

The Content Studio

One of the most lucrative—and trustworthy—ways for publishers to take advantage of the native craze is to help develop the content themselves rather than simply run a brand's pre-existing content, but to do that it needs those all-important storytellers. And to find them, marketing and sales departments will likely be turning to the people being laid-off from newsrooms.

If you're a journalist still managing to live in denial about the future of native advertising, you need look no further than the *New York Times* for a reality check. In 2013 the *Times* announced a full content studio (a department devoted to creating branded content). In April of 2014 Digiday—which has its own content studio—took "A look inside publishers' content studios" including at the *New York Times* and the *Wall Street Journal.* With 12 full-time staff, the *Times* was betting on the quality of its crew to be a big draw for brands. Ricardo Bilton wrote for Digiday, "Kaylee King-Balentine, its director of video branded content, for example, is an Emmy award winner. Other staffers include Melanie Deziel, formerly native ad products manager at the Huffington Post, and former Slate art director Michael Ryterband."

"We're replicating the kind of work that gets done in a newsroom," Meredith Kopit Levien, executive vice president of advertising at the *Times,* told Bilton. While not every piece of native advertising at the *Times* or elsewhere is a success, several years later, the *Times* has worked with many brands to create great content. Let's take a closer look at one in particular.

Look at Figure 4.2 carefully. Do you see the disclaimer? Right there above the headline and below the *Times* logo is a small notice advising readers that this is a paid post (in this case, sponsored by Netflix and *Orange Is the New Black*). But the rest of the content is better than most of what you'll read elsewhere on the web—and does not stand out as subpar on the *Times'* site. The article is accompanied by video interviews with female prison inmates and only mentions *Orange Is the New Black* in so far as it references an op-ed from Piper Kerman—the author of the book the series is based on—which addressed the problem of the lack of federal prisons for women. At the bottom of the page there is a banner ad for the show.

Figure 4.2 A screenshot of the *New York Times'* "Women Inmates" story, which is widely agreed to be one of the best examples of what branded content can be.

This is an example of exactly what native advertising—and content marketing—can and should be. It's informative. It's entertaining. It's clearly marked. And most importantly, it raises awareness about the show without the hard sell.

The author of the article is Melanie Deziel, whose title is branded content editor and social media strategist for the *New York Times.* If you follow her career back through The Huffington Post, you'll find that she started out in more traditional journalism jobs—beginning on the campus newspaper of my alma mater, The University of Connecticut, and interning for *The Day of New London* and *Rolling Stone* before working her way up to blogging for The Huffington Post.

The article was front and center in a now infamous tirade by John Oliver on his HBO show *Last Week Tonight.* While Oliver pointed to the "Women Inmates" story as being just about the best that native advertising has to offer, he also dredged up some more controversial examples.

"Ads are baked into content like chocolate chips into a cookie. Except, it's actually more like raisins into a cookie—because nobody fucking wants them there," Oliver said of native advertising, and pointed to such native advertising snafus as the Scientology ad in the *Atlantic* that got the media world buzzing (in an angry hornets sort of way). The post was titled "David Miscavige Leads Scientology to Milestone Year" and spurred such headlines as this one from Gawker: "The *Atlantic* is Now Publishing Bizarre, Blatant Scientology Propaganda as 'Sponsored Content'." (See Figure 4.3.) Obviously this didn't go over quite as well as the *Orange Is the New Black* piece.

In fact, the Scientology ad caused such a stir that the *Atlantic* eventually pulled it and issued a statement:

"We screwed up. It shouldn't have taken a wave of constructive criticism—but it has—to alert us that we've made a mistake, possibly several mistakes. We now realize that as we explored new forms of digital advertising, we failed to update the policies that must govern the decisions we make along the way. It's safe to say that we are thinking a lot more about these policies after running this ad than we did beforehand. In the meantime, we have decided to withdraw the ad until we figure all of this out. We remain committed to and enthusiastic about innovation in digital advertising, but acknowledge—sheepishly—that we got ahead of ourselves. We are sorry, and we're working very hard to put things right."

What this incident illustrates to me is just how new this whole industry really is—or, at least, how new this incarnation is. Notice that the *Atlantic* makes no mention of abandoning native advertising or branded content. Instead it simply acknowledges that, like many media outlets, it is still playing catch up. Publishers are desperate to bring in new, significant forms of revenue and for many that means publishing native ads—but it doesn't, and shouldn't mean abandoning your ethics—and the industry is still working out the kinks.

According to a HubSpot survey of 425 random internet users, 72.8 percent of internet users who have read sponsored content believe it has equal or greater value as nonsponsored content on the same website. Publishers should take note of this statistic, but not just because of the revenue opportunities that it presents. Right now consumers trust native advertising, but if publishers and brands aren't careful to maintain that trust, native ads may go the way of banners and become just one more form of advertising that consumers ignore.

Figure 4.3 This screenshot from Gawker.com is just one example of the derision the *Atlantic* earned for a sponsored post about Scientology.

Maintaining your audience's trust is paramount to the success of native advertising and content marketing, and it is up to publishers and content creators to set up boundaries and standards that assure that quality and trust do not have to suffer in the face of changing publishing realities. Establishing your own content studios, putting journalists you trust in charge, and setting up clear boundaries is the first step on the road to success.

In fact, companies would be smart to take a cue from Soledad O'Brien, well-known journalist and founder of Starfish Media Group. O'Brien has been making documentaries since her departure from CNN, and I had the chance to hear her speak at Content All-Stars in New York. She touched on the challenge of creating sponsored content without compromising editorial integrity. She pointed to a new documentary she was working on about girls that happens to be sponsored by Cover Girl. As she puts it, "You have to four-wall it." In other words, make it very clear from the beginning that the sponsor is simply underwriting the content and that editorial control is up to you. This may drive some potential sponsors away, but maintaining your integrity for the long-term should be of the utmost importance—even in the face of short-term gains. Because, as Anil Dash, co-founder and CEO of ThinkUp, said at the same event, "You can mortgage trust and reputation, but you can only do it once."

Of course content marketing isn't all about native advertising and sponsored posts. B2B publishers have relied on distributing vendor white papers and delivering leads back to the advertisers as one of their staple sources of income for decades. This familiar form of marketing is evolving, and today, more than ever, great storytellers are needed to make this content compelling—otherwise a whole new kind of blindness might set in among readers.

Chapter 5

Journalists and Marketing— A Match Made in Content Heaven

Journalists leaving the newsroom to find jobs on the other side of the communications table is nothing new. For decades, reporters seeking better pay and more job security have turned to careers in public relations—otherwise known as "the dark side." It's a natural fit, even if journalists resist the change. Who knows how to pitch a story better than an ex-journo? Who knows how to get an editor's attention—without pestering them so much as to destroy the relationship—better than a former reporter? These skills, along with an ability to find, research, and execute a great story, make journalists—or at least some of them—natural content marketers.

Of course, it can be hard to convince someone who spent their time in J-school dreaming of winning a Pulitzer Prize, or becoming the next Woodward or Bernstein, that they should ditch their dreams and start selling Pepsi (or tractors, or cars, or whatever widget you can think of). No one wants to be a sellout—not even the perpetually underemployed and hapless Hannah Horvath. Fans of the HBO show *Girls* may remember Hannah's brief stint as a brand journalist in the third season. Hannah found herself gainfully employed, and able to pay her rent for the first time, but her dreams of being a true artist got in the way. Even though her job writing native advertising pieces at a magazine had her interviewing the likes of none other than diva Patty Lupone about her experience with an osteoporosis medication, Hannah wasn't satisfied, and ended up blowing up in a staff meeting (her attempt at purposely getting fired) in a fit of artistic rage.

And Hannah isn't even a journalist!

In the real world, though, writers may want to think twice before putting their principles before their pocketbooks. “The internet is thirsty for talented journalists. Brand gigs pay well, are getting more interesting and free of stigma,” says Contently co-founder Shane Snow. “Part of the reason the stigma is disappearing is because brands have realized that in order for people to like their content, it has to be objectively good and free of deception—which is what scared journalists in the past about working with brands. A lot more journalists are pouring into content marketing now than even a couple of years ago.”

Back in 2009, David Meerman Scott started making his case. His open letter to journalists on his WebInkNow blog, entitled “You have an amazing career opportunity on the Dark Side,” encouraged writers to take the jobs he had urged marketing departments to create. Scott explained, “I’m not talking about PR and media relations here. This isn’t about writing press releases and trying to get your former colleagues to write or broadcast about you. Instead, I’m talking about creating stories as you are now, but for a corporation, government agency, nonprofit, or educational institution instead. You’ve probably not seriously considered that there are potential employers outside of media companies.”

You can do the same work in a new industry, according to Scott, and feel just as proud of the product you create. “I take issue with the term ‘brand journalism,’ however,” says Snow. “What brands are doing, by and large, is not journalism. It’s information and entertainment. It can still be honest, but let’s not conflate what they’re doing with the Fourth Estate.”

Not everyone would agree with Snow, though it certainly isn’t an unusual opinion. Some content marketers are starting to fight back against the notion that what they do isn’t—at least sometimes—legitimate journalism. In a Lush Digital Media post called “Brand Journalism: Why the Faulty Arguments Need to End” the Lush team writes, “Does sports reporting favour the hometown team? Does entertainment reporting court local celebrities? Do local news stations give equal coverage to rival cities? That doesn’t mean those reporters are not journalists or working in journalism. Like sports, entertainment or local interest stories, brand journalism is just another flavour of journalism.”

EContent: *I'm still not sure how you came to content marketing. Can you tell me a bit about "Joe before the CMI?" In other words, how did you come to be interested in content marketing in the first place?*

Joe Pulizzi: While I've been in publishing of some sort for a long time (mock newsletter creation as a kid, yearbook editor), I got my start in content marketing at Penton Media, headquartered in Cleveland, Ohio. Penton is the largest independent business media company in North America. You probably wouldn't know any of its 150 publications and brands unless you were in the trades like mechanical systems, manufacturing, or organic foods. I joined Penton in 2000 in the custom media department and took over the department in 2001. Basically, our job was to work with Penton advertisers that didn't want to advertise but wanted help creating their own content such as custom magazines, newsletters, webinars, or white papers. We served as an in-house publishing agency for longer-form content creation.

I cut my teeth at Penton, had some amazing mentors, and was able to see the shift from paid media to owned media firsthand from 2000 to 2007 as search engine optimization, social media, and lead generation programs were nothing without first having a content marketing strategy.

Excerpted from "Q&A: Joe Pulizzi, Founder, Content Marketing Institute" (EContentmag.com)

We've already heard from some of the industry's foremost experts that the best content marketers come from trade publications. The difference between covering an industry and creating content marketing for its players is negligible. In many ways, done right, creating content marketing should be like working for a newsroom with better funding. Again, I defer to Scott to explain:

"Please realize that I am not advocating the old-school 'advertorial' model. Advertorials such as those late-night cable TV shows about a product or the full-page product information 'reports' found in trade journals is not what I'm talking about here. The idea of using your journalistic skills should be to educate and inform, not to overtly sell products." The content marketing industry is still evolving. Surely there are marketing departments that still don't get it but that's changing—and you can help be a part of that change.

In "The Editor's Guide to Working with Brands," which Ryan Galloway wrote for Contently, the author asserted that "Ten years ago, if you told your newsroom colleagues that some of the industry's most gifted editors would start abandoning their gigs at marquee media brands to join beverage companies, software providers, or a service that delivers pet treats to your home, you would've been laughed out of the room (and possibly prescribed some heavy-duty pharmaceuticals). Today, however, having a great editorial leader on staff isn't just helpful for brands—it's table stakes."

But don't be fooled, there will be some challenges to making a big career shift. Snow warns, "Two things: owning and cultivating your personal brand (which helps you sell you), and getting savvy about the business results of the work you're doing. Because there is increasing competition for audience attention on the web, it has become even more critical to produce content that is engaging. Successful brand publishers pay more attention to the way they're building relationships with readers, not just how many page views they're getting. And relationships correlate to ROI, which is the ultimate goal of content marketing."

The Storyteller Shortage

It's hard to imagine that marketing departments are still struggling to find great content creators. After years of experts advocating for brands to hire journalists you would think more journalist and marketers would be connecting, but according to a post by Gabe Rosenberg on Contently's Content Strategist site, that just isn't the case. Referring to a OneSpot infographic called "The Human Factor in Content Marketing," he wrote, "Resources are a big problem for content marketers: Sixty-nine percent feel their greatest challenge

The Best Content Marketers Around

In 2015 David Griner put together a list of "10 Branded Content Masters Who Make It OK to Love Marketing" for *AdWeek*, listing the people who set the branded content bar high—and give journalists entering the field something to aspire to.

1. Wil Tidman, Head of Production, Go Pro
2. Melissa Rosenthal, VP of Creative Services, BuzzFeed
3. David Beebe, VP of Content Marketing, Marriott International
4. Ryan Rimsnider, Senior Manager of Social Strategy, Taco Bell
5. Catherine Patterson, SVP and Executive Producer, McCann NY
6. Katrina Craigwell, Director of Global Content and Programming, General Electric
7. James Percelay and Michael Krivicka, Co-Founders, Thinkmodo
8. Tina Cervera, SVP and Executive Creative Director, VaynerMedia
9. Chis Lindland, Founder and CEO, Betabrand
10. Joe Chernov, VP of Content, HubSpot

is lack of time, while half still struggle with producing enough content to engage their target audience. That's evident by the fact that only one in three content marketers are creating multiple content assets to distribute each week."

To anyone used to working on a daily—or even weekly—news deadline, this low output must seem laughable. I suspect that the vice grip of corporate communications may be strangling content output. Some companies still want to send every piece of content through a lengthy and arcane approval process rather than just setting standards and guidelines for their employees and trusting they will follow the rules. But more importantly those marketers are reporting a lack of time and resources, which says to me that many marketing departments still don't have a staff member devoted solely to creating compelling content. This leads to 62 percent of marketing departments relying on agencies and freelancers to create at least some of their content—and 78.3 percent plan on growing their team by one to three people within a year.

That's a lot of jobs!

Opportunities already exist for journalists willing to take the leap, and all signs point to continued growth in this industry. The public's hunger for content isn't slowing down, and consumers care less and less about the source of that content. So if you're already thinking about crossing the divide, now may be the perfect time.

Uncovering Content Marketing Jobs

To hear our experts tell it, every decent journalist should be having their doors beaten down by marketing departments desperate for a good storyteller. Of course, that's not exactly the case, and there is one obstacle to finding full-time content marketing positions that keeps coming up. Many companies just don't know what to call the jobs they are advertising.

Australia-based content marketer Jonathan Crossfield says companies don't necessarily have standard descriptions or job titles. While one company may be advertising for a copy writer, another may be looking for a content manager, and the next might want a content strategist—but the tasks and duties associated with each of these may be screaming "content marketer." So if you're looking for a job in the industry, he encourages you to dig around. "There are roles that you can adapt your skills to," he says.

There Is No "Dark Side"

Journalists occupy a special place in our society. They are a type of interpreter—finding and telling the important stories. It's their job to sort through the constant stream of information for the bits that matter and root out the secrets no one wants you to know about.

But let's face it, most journalists aren't embedded with rebels in Syria or working with the next Edward Snowden. No, far more are working in trade magazines, reviewing food or electronics, covering celebrity gossip, and sitting through town council meetings. This is the reality of many reporters and writers across the globe. What they do is important, but it isn't always all that different from what their content marketer brethren are up to.

Even if you are working at the *New York Times*, the hallowed territory between church and state is eroding. Native advertising (and therefore content marketing) is becoming a part of your work-life reality. More importantly, many content marketing gigs are more nuanced and satisfying than you might ever imagine. You don't have to sign up with a big name brand to sell soft drinks or shoes—the opportunities available to you are so much more varied than that.

Michelle Manafy's early career helped shape her for her latest position as the editorial director at Digital Content Next (DCN—formerly the Online Publishers Association).

"I promote the magic of media. ... My mission is to champion the content people love," says Manafy, whose long career in journalism saw her working for everyone from the *Village Voice* to Access Intelligence—and, of course, *EContent*. And as many journalists who have ventured into the realm of content marketing have figured out, the transition from journalism to marketing requires individuals to rethink the way they do business.

"The biggest difference out of the gate ... is that you don't look for the news," Manafy says. These days, her job is more about supporting the DCN marketing team's goals than it is about breaking news. "When you work with highly skilled marketers," she says, "they build storylines that are going to be their campaigns for the year." The content Manafy creates now has to support those campaigns—although that doesn't mean she completely turns off her journalistic instincts.

"I still try to bring content back around to the big trends, but it's turned on its side," she says. One of the hardest things about this, though, is ignoring the news.

For a more general audience, Manafy might have covered net neutrality, but because her organization's role is to represent the interests of its members—and those interests aren't necessarily aligned with one another on a topic such as net neutrality—she avoids covering such topics.

The other big change for Manafy has been the pace. She's used to the pace of a newsroom, where content is constantly being churned out. But in the world of brand journalism, quality is more important than quantity. This has turned out to be a bit of a blessing, because as Manafy prepared to launch DCN's content hub, she had an important realization: No one pitches stories to content marketers. Instead of spending every morning weeding through dozens of pitches in her inbox, Manafy now reaches out to her member organizations looking for stories that help support DCN's chosen themes.

"I'm going to have be proactive because I'm not even on their PR lists," says Manafy. Until she can forge a more conventional press relationship with these companies, she has set up monitors and alerts to make sure she isn't missing any initiatives from the companies she's tasked with covering. Content marketing experts have long been urging brands to hire reporters, and many journalists—such as Manafy—are seizing that opportunity. However, they may need to keep a few things in mind before jumping at the first job that comes along.

"Here's what I think you can bring to the craft of marketing from the craft of journalism: passion for your subject matter," Manafy says. "When you look at what you're going to be 'selling,' be sure you care about it. Be sure it's something you can align your personal brand with. You aren't just punching a time clock." In other words, in order to create the kind of great content that good content marketing demands, you need to be passionate about your subject matter. So whatever you do, don't settle.

We can learn a lot from Manafy's example, but there is one main takeaway that I hope journalists will absorb: If you decide to make the switch to content marketing, you can still do what you love and create content that you're proud of.

When we talk about brands—and, by extension, brand journalists—we tend to think of giant corporations, selling products we may or may not use or believe in, but there is an entire world out there beyond those corporate gigs. In Manafy's case, she made the switch from writing about the content and media world for trade publications to writing about the same subjects from a different angle for a trade organization. She continues to provide valuable content to, more or less, the same audience.

Trade organizations are a great place for journalists to look for content marketing positions, but it doesn't stop there. Nonprofits of all sorts stand to benefit uniquely from this kind of outreach. Often strapped for cash and working with practically nonexistent advertising budgets, nonprofits need someone adept at creating compelling content that can bring them the attention that they can't afford to buy through traditional channels.

According to the *2014 Nonprofit Content Marketing Benchmarks, Budgets, and Trends—North America* from CMI, 92 percent of content marketing professionals use content marketing—and, more importantly, it's working. Kentico Software delved into the effects of content marketing on charitable giving for part of its ongoing Digital Research series. The study found that "while visual content is commonly credited for amplifying many of today's digital marketing efforts, when it comes to charities, donors are much more likely to respond to personal stories (35%) and statistics (32%)."

"While charities continue to face an uphill battle in attracting new donors, our survey suggests the right digital content can encourage greater generosity among repeat donors," said Kentico CEO and founder Petr Palas in a press release. "Regardless of the cause or need, nonprofit sites need to combine the human and emotional elements along with the hard facts that show how widespread the problem might be."

Remember that list of the 25 most influential content marketing brands from a few chapters ago? One of those brands was none other than ALS, which raised more than $100 million with its Ice Bucket Challenge. Everyone from your neighbor to Matt Damon got involved—and Damon got a two-for-one good deed in, using the Ice Bucket challenge to raise awareness for his own organization, Water.org, by using water from his toilet to dump over his head. The success enjoyed by ALS came through user-generated content, but it remains a great example of what content marketing can do for small, nonprofit organizations that are short on budget but long on creativity.

Of course not every nonprofit is going to convince millions of people to dump ice water over their heads, but nonprofits tend to have especially compelling stories to tell. Imagine, just for a moment, that you found a job working with a local organization that provides shelter and job training for the homeless. A good journalist could find untold numbers of stories to tell for this kind of company. A new one literally walks through the door every day. From redemption stories about the people the organization helps to infographics using statistics about homelessness to profiles of the people who work for the organization, the content possibilities are endless. And I'd be willing to bet the blog posts, infographics, and videos a content marketer could create for an organization like this would do far more good—and be far more satisfying—than all the town council coverage in the world. Take for instance the example from NoMore.org (see Figure 5.1), which features the personal stories of domestic abuse survivors.

Once you decide to make the switch, though, Snow has some advice on how to get started on building your portfolio. "Do what you do best: find stories and pitch them," he says. "I'd recommend starting to freelance for some brands and slowly shifting the balance of your full time work to freelance. Or, honestly, just look at the job pages on brands you care about. Nearly every major brand is hiring for content marketing roles of some sort."

Whether you end up going to work for a Fortune 500 company, a government agency, or a nonprofit, the potential for content marketing positions is limitless. It may take some time to find the one that's right for you, but the beauty of these positions is that no two are the same—and in many cases, the position will be yours to shape.

Figure 5.1 A screenshot from NoMore.org, which uses content marketing to spread awareness about domestic violence.

The Faces of Content Marketing

Nancy Davis Kho has been writing the "Faces of EContent" column for years. Through the years she has interviewed dozens of professionals in the digital content industry, and over the past few years more and more content marketing titles have been appearing in her column. For the July/August 2014 issue of *EContent*, Kho talked to Amanda Maksymiw, content marketing manager at Lattice. Maksymiw described her typical day this way: "I'll poke around on social media and the web to uncover conversations about data-driven marketing and sales and predictive analytics, in addition to looking for inspiration for content outside of the B2B tech space…I maintain an ongoing relationship with industry influencers, so I try to share interesting content with them on a monthly basis." Of course there is plenty of actual content creation happening as well.

In another installment of "Faces of EContent," Kho interviewed John Forrester, social media community manager and brand

Questions to Answer Before Becoming a Full-Time Content Marketer

Can you write about this topic every day? If you're a trade journalist chances are you're already writing about one topic on a regular basis. But before you accept any content marketing position be sure you can be passionate about the content you'll be creating.

What is the editorial process like? Adjusting to the difference between working in a newsroom and working in a marketing department will be your biggest challenge. So before you take the job make sure you understand how the editorial process will work and where the boundary lines are.

What are the goals for the content marketing program? How will they be measured? Your success as a content marketer will be measured differently than your success as a journalist, and you should know before you accept a position exactly how that will be.

journalist at Arnold Worldwide. Unlike Maksymiw, Forrester works in an agency setting, so his days look a little different. Kho wrote, "'I'm responsible for researching, reporting, and writing long-form editorial content for NewBalance.com and ensuring that each piece makes its way to the client through Arnold's editorial process,' Forrester says. On a monthly basis, he assists in the development of content deliverables, from long-form articles on the brand's website to bite-size graphics distributed through social channels. Forrester says, 'Beyond editorial production, I also keep an eye on running and sneaker head publications and online communities to see what direction their content is going.'"

Kho also interviewed Ernie Smith, who had the tricky title of "social media journalist" for TMG, a content marketing firm. He worked closely with the American Society of Association Executives.

Smith told Kho, "I work directly with ASAE staff in shaping the tone and the style of the content, which is largely curated with daily blog posts and a strong focus on visuals. I design my own infographics and illustrations, I help post to social media, I played a key role in designing the look of the newsletter which we publish Monday through Friday—and a key role in writing it, too."

As you can see, not all content marketing jobs are created equal. Duties and responsibilities will vary, just like with any job. It will be up to you to find the right position to fit your skills, but the good news is that no matter what your interest or skill level, there is almost certainly a job for you.

Getting Your Content Marketing Education

Let's assume I've convinced you that transitioning from journalism to content marketing is the right path for you. You may still be confused about the difference between being a journalist and being a brand journalist. Many of your skills will transfer seamlessly to the world of content marketing, but there is no denying that adjustments will need to be made. And a little training may be in order.

"The gap between content marketing awareness and good content marketing execution is not surprising. It's something we run into every day at the Institute—what we call the digital skills gap," Online Marketing Institute founder and CEO Aaron Kahlow said in a press release about Forrester's "Compare Your B2B Content Marketing Maturity." "There simply aren't enough trained content marketers to do the legwork. But the imperative for education is here and seen across the board, from entry level to CMO."

You're off to the right start if you're reading this book, but as the need for content marketers grows, so too does the industry around them. Companies and organizations are seeing the need for content marketing education, and they are rushing to fill the gap. Of course you can count on the content marketing experts to produce plenty of educational content. The CMI puts on Content Marketing World each September in Cleveland, Ohio, to bring together thousands of marketers for four days of intensive education.

If you're in need of more formal education, you can find it through Copyblogger. The site has quickly grown into a major resource for content marketing education like ebooks, advice-filled posts, seminars, webinars, and great newsletters. More recently it has offered a Content Certification Program, which includes four weeks of in-depth coursework on content strategy, marketing materials to help students find more clients, and the opportunity to eventually apply for certification. The CMI offers a similar program which consists of 19 hours of online instructional content for $995 per year.

I hesitate to even put the name of these programs down in writing because it seems that every time I turn around, another content marketing course is popping up and no list will ever be comprehensive. But rest assured, there are plenty of options out there.

Chapter 6

Lessons from Brand Journalists

People from diverse personal and professional backgrounds are making a living as content marketers from one end of the globe to the other. I interviewed many of them for *Inside Content Marketing*, and I found it interesting, though not surprising, that their personal experiences echoed the findings and advice of researchers and experts. In this chapter these content marketers share their experience and expertise to help future content marketers—and the brands and publishers that hire them—learn how to be successful.

Sarah Mitchell: A Journey Along the Content Spectrum

"Friction between journalists and marketers is on the rise. Traditional journalists are railing against native advertising but don't necessarily distinguish between advertising and marketing. Others insist journalists are better suited for content marketing than copywriters. As someone who possesses both marketing and journalism credentials, I can see the sense in arguments on both sides." Sarah Mitchell wrote these words on her site GlobalCopywriting.com in a post titled "The Difference Between Journalism And Brand Journalism (And Why It Matters)." Mitchell does, indeed, have an interesting background that took her all along the content spectrum—and she has plenty to teach brands and writers alike.

"My big advantage in content marketing was starting in business. I understand the business mindset, what they're trying to accomplish and how hard it can be for them to describe their products and services in an objective manner," Mitchell says. "Business is all about push marketing. Having spent five years in a direct sales role, I was very clear on what that outbound message was like. Still,

I pulled on my experience in the sales role and found the hard sell approach didn't work for me."

It was as a sales person that Mitchell started seeing how good content could benefit the sales funnel. "I was much more of a consultative salesperson and I first started developing my own content at that time," she says. "The marketing collateral was heavy-handed and I knew my prospects and customers were responding more to my technical expertise and practical experience. They didn't trust marketing, they trusted experience."

But after years in the business world, Mitchell decided to make a shift. She became a journalist, working at publications like *KL American Magazine* before eventually becoming a freelancer. Mitchell says, "When I moved into journalism, it was a pure pleasure to write objectively. I loved opinion pieces but only from a journalistic standpoint. I actually loved having to research to support my opinions. After those years in sales, it was wonderful to be objective on a subject."

Like many freelance journalists, the sporadic and not always lucrative gigs eventually inspired Mitchell to make a move to copywriting. "The freelance journalism gig was great, and I still freelance when I can, but I had this vision I would write case studies and white papers for organizations to help with their marketing efforts. What I quickly found out was that most businesses didn't have good writing/reporting skills on their staff," she says. Just like the studies I've quoted throughout this book, Mitchell found that most companies were lacking in the content marketing department.

"They had a hard time writing objectively. They didn't know how to tell a story. Everything was boring as dirt or just plain painful to read. This was in the beginning of 2009 when content marketing really started to gain traction in the U.S.A. I was reading Joe Pulizzi, Mike Stelzner, Casey Hibbard, Jay Baer, Peter Bowerman, Jamie Wallace, Michele Linn, Steve Slaunwhite, Stephanie Tilton, Ardith Albee, Jonathan Crossfield—all these folks kept talking about the importance of quality content and tamping down the hard sell messages," Mitchell says. "I knew from my work in sales that this was absolutely the way to go. It was in 2009 that I began to realize all these different products—blog posts, white papers, case studies, etc.—were tactics to content marketing. I was writing about content marketing on my own blog but never calling it anything. It was half way through 2009 before I started talking about the broader discipline."

Sarah Mitchell on Content Strategy

Strategy is everything, it guides what you're going to do, how much you're going to spend and how you're going to measure success. You're building long-term business assets when you create original, high-quality content so it's important to understand what assets are needed in your company. I write and speak about content strategy quite often. A strategy needs to be based on business goals, not some other frothy metric as defined by the marketing department or an outside service provider. If your content is not moving people towards purchase, it's a waste of time no matter how popular it is. A content marketing strategy should address three components (or tactics) of content marketing:

Original content

Social Media

Search Engine Optimization (SEO)

These days Sarah Mitchell is the associate director of Lush Digital Media, where she helps companies create content marketing strategies. She is also a consultant and the editor of the Australian edition of Content Marketing Institute's (CMI) magazine *Chief Content Officer*. Despite the content marketing boom, Mitchell says she doesn't see too many of her journalist friends jumping ship and coming over to the marketing side. "I wish more were making the switch because business needs good writing, people who can tell a story, and who can write to a word count and a deadline," she says. "It also needs people that can crank out the copy quickly. Journalists are all good at that sort of thing. Not only do I recommend them making the switch, I actively recruit them."

Mitchell is realistic about the difference between journalism and brand journalism, and her advice to prospective content marketers reflects that. "The writing has to be persuasive. That doesn't mean objectivity isn't important because it is. It does mean that you're helping a reader draw a conclusion," she says. "Journalists rail against this idea but it's been happening since the beginning of journalism. You see it most often in how papers align themselves politically. There have always been Democratic and Republican newspapers, liberal and conservative, labor and liberal—however you want to dice it. Lastly, and I wrote about this on my blog, content marketing requires a call to action in all their content. You have to ask for the conversion. You have to suggest the reader do something."

This may be one of the biggest sticking points for purists, but it's all about walking that fine line between marketing and advertising—between suggesting and overt selling. That being said, the content doesn't have to suffer to meet your end goals. "The last thing they should know is that if they're working at the right company, they can employ all their journalistic skills, write what they want, and make a good wage doing it," Mitchell says. "Not all

Sarah Mitchell on Hiring a Journalist

The first important thing is to write a detailed brief and include the call to action. The journalist has to know the goal of the story before writing and they have to understand what the reader is expected to do.

I would absolutely get writing examples. I've worked with journalists that couldn't string a sentence but they had no qualms about asking for a very high hourly rate. All I think is that they must have worked with good editors in the past.

I always do a test project the first time I work with someone. Don't assign six stories; assign one and see if you can work together. There's an English expression, 'horses for courses.' Not all journalists are good at writing every kind of content.

brands let journalists be journalists but business is waking up to that. Some of the best content marketers I know are journalists."

Even under the best of circumstances, you may still find resistance within the ranks of a marketing department. This is why, if you're looking for an in-house position with a brand or organization, you ask the right questions in the beginning. If you decide to freelance, you may be a bit more at the mercy of the hiring company. "As a consultant, all I can do is give my advice and back it up with examples and research. The marketing team ultimately makes the decision. In an organization, the content marketing team should be part of the marketing team so I hope no editorial issues arise," Mitchell says. "A good example I see all the time is that business wants content to be very 'me' focused. Everything is about them, what they do, what they want. The modern consumer wants none of that. They're looking to business to help them make decisions. They don't care about the company; they care about how the company can help them. One of the big changes I always make is to remove all the 'I' and 'We' language and flip it to 'You' or 'Your'. It's a hard one for a lot of people to get their head around."

Of course this is all the more reason that brands need people like Sarah Mitchell to help execute their content marketing strategy. Without the help of storytellers, companies' content marketing will continue to languish, forever suffering from a lack of expertise and true understanding of what makes great content.

Sarah Mitchell's Content Marketing Stars

"Tourism Australia is knocking them dead, especially because they're getting so much user generated content (UGC). It's easy to get people excited about travel and holidays, though, so I always look for examples where it's not so easy," Mitchell says. With that in mind, she points to LTV from Lush Digital Media. She says, "Their roots are in video production and it shows in this series of interviews with thought leaders from all different sectors: business, sports, medicine, technology, property, etc."

There's one more company that's wowing Mitchell right now. "Black Milk Clothing does an awesome job on the storytelling side of things. I wrote about them in... *CCO* magazine which turned out

Figure 6.1 A screenshot of Black Milk Clothing's page on Vimeo.

to be the cover story," she says. [See Figure 6.1.] "They have lots of user-generated content but also put a lot of effort into all their communications. Their gift vouchers are a long story putting the customer in the center of the action. Their receipts have a couple paragraphs of thanks."

Jonathan Crossfield: The Second Act Storyteller

Early in my conversation with Jonathan Crossfield, he challenged every notion journalists hold dear about their chosen profession. "Journalists are still seeing an ethical gulf for writing for a supposedly independent publication and for a brand," he says. "Is there such a thing as a supposedly independent and unbiased publication? Everyone has an angle…If you're writing for Rupert Murdoch there is a company line."

Crossfield also reiterated something I heard time and again while researching this book. "Journalists think their personal ethics or personal opinions are going to be over ridden or compromised, and that's not the case when [content marketing] is done right," he says.

Crossfield came to his career in content marketing in a roundabout fashion. After 10 years as an office manager he decided to go back to his passion: writing. "I got a job for a brand in their marketing department where they wanted a writer," he says. "They were just about to publish a custom magazine which was going to be in news agents, so it was a classic content marketing ploy." Funnily enough, a column in that branded magazine led to Crossfield winning his first journalism award. While the people who hand out awards—whoever that may be—are not distinguishing between content marketing and journalism when it comes to great content, journalists are still resisting the crossover. Crossfield sees it all the time.

He says, "I was running workshops with a publisher in Sydney, and even though they now have a content marketing department, and they're doing a lot more branded content…the journalism team that works on the various magazines and publications still sat there saying 'For ethical reasons, I don't want to do anything that's been sponsored or has a brand attached to it…' They're still very protective of their turf."

With these kinds of attitudes still pervasive in the content industry, it's no wonder that Crossfield's clients often have the same complaints we've heard in study after study. They can't find the right writers. They tell him, "We need writers but we also need writers that know our industry or vertical." That can be hard to find when journalists are still taking a hard line against content marketing.

Many of our experts have said the place to look for your next content marketer is in your industry trade press, but Crossfield himself defied that advice at the start of his career. He went to work for a brand magazine, which focused on technology and web hosting but knew almost nothing about the topic. "The first time I heard the word SEO was in the actual job interview," he says. "I must have fudged my way through it because I had absolutely no clue.…The level of expertise I had was very small. But the way I work…was I just immersed myself in the topic for the first 3 months I was there." In the end, Crossfield chalks getting that first job up to his skill as a writer and not so much to his technical expertise.

This was the early days of the branded content renaissance—2007 or so—and Crossfield says he considers himself lucky to have gotten his start in the early days, when he could still learn his new trade on the fly.

Describing his career today is such a difficult task that I'll just leave that up to him (and his website): "He calls himself a storyteller, mainly because it fits on a business card better than a long list of writer, marketer, journalist, copywriter, social media consultant, speaker and blogger. To use any other job title would be to pigeonhole him inaccurately. But storytelling underpins everything he does, from copywriting an EDM to planning a content strategy to scribbling ghost stories in those rare spare moments." In short, he's one of the most highly regarded and in-demand content marketers on the scene—and was in the midst of researching his own book when I spoke with him.

Despite his own experience, Crossfield still says that expertise is important to being a good content marketer—and you can often see the problems that a lack of subject matter knowledge creates in agency settings. The in-house writers at marketing agencies are often junior writers right out of college. "The problem that agencies have…is it's not always going to be a perfect fit as a result," Crossfield says. "Particularly when they have an in-house pool of writers…they have to have a lot of expertise across a smaller pool, or less experienced writers." In these cases editors often only have a few more years of experience than their writers and, Crossfield says, simply end up getting a list of topics from clients, quickly researching them online to see what competitors are doing, and then assigning the articles to writers—who, in turn, research the topics through Google. This process results in content that is just a rehash of what other companies and experts in the space have already said. Crossfield calls it, "Content marketing for the sake of content marketing." In that situation, he adds, "No one wins except the agency."

As the old saying goes, if you want something done right, you have to do it yourself—and that includes building a content marketing department from the ground up with the right people.

Finding the right people to head up your content initiative may mean persuading the right journalists to sign up for a career change. "Working for a brand is not switching to the dark side," says

Jonathan Crossfield on Building Boundaries and Setting Expectations

In "The Human Factor in Content Marketing" OneSpot asserts "that only one in three content marketers are creating multiple content assets to distribute each week." To the average journalist this is shocking, but anyone who has ever worked under the constraints of a corporate communications department might understand.

Crossfield found the statistic surprising, but not wholly unbelievable—even if he is personally pumping out at least one blog post per day.

He often gets questions from workshop attendees about how to deal with overbearing legal departments. "Legal wants to approve every tweet and it's a three day process....What content marketers need to be better at doing is negotiating those things in advance," he says.

Crossfield suggests you have to lay the groundwork up front to prevent unnecessary interference down the road. Get your editorial calendar approved in advance, and agree on acceptable language and messaging so that every blog post doesn't need to be vetted before it posts.

Crossfield. "You can have all the same ethical values that you had before, just covering one particular niche topic."

"There's a lot of myth out there that somehow [brand journalism] is not journalism," he adds. "And I dispute that." He cites a fear of the unknown and peer pressure from colleagues as "the barriers that journalists need to overcome to realize it's all part of the same pie."

Jonathan Crossfield's Content Marketing Stars

There is one piece of content marketing that, surprisingly, didn't come up more often during my research, but that really caught Jonathan Crossfield's eye. SunGard Availability Services provides

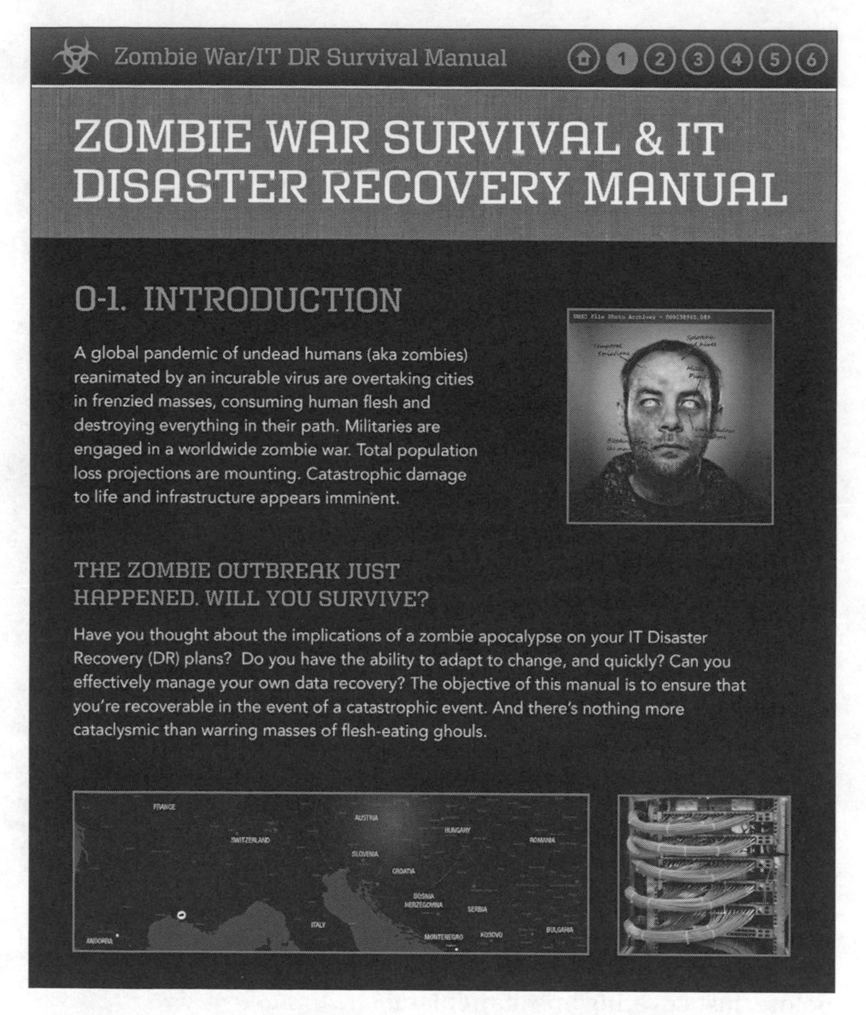

Figure 6.2 A screenshot of "Zombie War Survival & IT Disaster Recovery Manual," which grabbed the attention of many in content marketing circles.

disaster recovery solutions for IT departments. Boring, right? So the company released "Zombie War Survival & IT Disaster Recovery Manual"—a white paper straight out of *The Walking Dead* (see Figure 6.2). "Content marketing doesn't need to be boring anymore," says Crossfield. He also likes that instead of writing a dry white paper aimed at the CEO, SunGard's content marketers understood the audience, which is actually "the IT guy, who is sitting at his desk in a *Walking Dead* t-shirt."

Crossfield also likes Workshifting.com from Citrix. "It's a content hub where all the articles are about how to work better in the modern age....It doesn't mention Citrix. It's just well-written content on topics that people would naturally come across when they're searching for 'how can I sync my documents better between my laptop and my smartphone?'"

Daniel Hatch: One Change After Another

Back in 2010, Daniel Hatch had never even heard of content marketing. "I'd spent more than a decade honing my craft as a journalist in print and radio newsrooms around my native Western Australia," he says. "Then all of a sudden one day I decided to pack it all in and go on an adventure. I moved to the U.K. in January 2011."

As so often happens, one change follows another, and things did not go quite as planned upon Hatch's arrival on his new continent. "Originally I planned to work for the newspapers here in London but I soon discovered how difficult it is to get a foot in the door," he says. "Or worse, if you do get a foot in the door, they want you to hire a car and sit outside Madonna's house all night until the lights go out and then go through her trash in search of a story. It's fair to say that wasn't for me."

Lucky for Hatch the internet has made the world a small place, because his new big break would come from the other side of the world, back in his home country. He says, "By total coincidence, just as I was starting to despair, I connected with Global Copywrite's Sarah Mitchell. We had been following each other on Twitter for a while and when we connected through LinkedIn as well she realized I might be at a loose end. She was snowed with work, had blogs that needed writing, and wondered if I wanted to give it a shot."

Hatch was in no position to be picky, but he also liked the idea of a good challenge—of trying something new. "Over time, the amount of work coming through from Sarah, and other agencies, began to grow. Soon I was helping out on some really big projects—and I was thoroughly enjoying the research aspect of the job as well as the writing," he says. "And before long I was lucky enough to be able to pick and choose what briefs I wanted to take: Lifestyle blogs for a developer, I would do; articles about cloud computing, I would not."

Hatch's example is a good one for journalists just starting to embark on a freelance content marketing career. At first you may have to take whatever jobs come your way, but if you build a solid reputation, you may soon have the luxury of picking and choosing the jobs you're interested in. "For me, the transition has been easy. It's just like journalism in a lot of ways. I still get to talk to people about what they're passionate about, share their stories, research, write, edit—all the stuff I've been trained to do," he says. "I could never have imagined that several years later I'd be a full-time freelancer and content marketing would make up a significant proportion of my income."

Hatch doesn't plan on leaving his journalism career behind. For him—and many other freelancers—being a journalist and being a brand journalist go hand in hand. In Hatch's case, the two disciplines are very much the same. "To some extent I approach them in the same way. And that's deliberate. My niche in content marketing—the thing that I can offer clients—is that I approach every story as a journalist would," he says. "So I research the topic thoroughly, I use various reliable sources of good information for each article, where I can I will conduct an actual interview with someone, and I write the piece in a 'newsy' fashion."

That doesn't mean the process, or even the goal, is exactly the same. In order to deliver quality content to clients, you need to understand where journalism and brand journalism differ. "Where it differs is that journalism really is meant to be 'without fear or favor.' Obviously, when you're writing for a client, a different prerogative comes into play," Hatch says. "When I write a content marketing article, I'm not necessarily trying to canvas all sides of a discussion as I would in a newspaper article. I don't have to."

That may raise the hackles of some journalists, but every reporter who crosses over and becomes a content marketer has to figure out where the ethical line is. "Shouldn't I have a problem with this ethically, you might ask? My response is 'why?' The reader is the person doing the research," Hatch says. "My article is just one stop on their journey. They'll read other articles and get other advice, too. I'm also not here to sell anything. The whole point of content marketing is to provide good information to the punters, without them feeling like they're being hustled. My job is just to impart that information as clearly, succinctly and helpfully as I can."

Daniel Hatch's Advice to Brands

If you want someone who can write well, fast and accurately, you can do no better. If you want a hard-worker who's good with deadlines, get a journalist.

But don't assume that a journalist will have all the skills you require. They won't. They need tutoring in the 'dark arts.' Teach them about content marketing. Give them the tools they need for a slightly different kind of writing.

And challenge them. Journalists are used to working in a highly competitive environment. They're brilliant idea generators. They get excited about telling good stories. They're used to leaping out of the office to go interview people. So don't just give them a computer and a stack of briefs—they'll get bored and, ultimately, you'll lose them.

As great as content marketing can be to help pay the bills, Hatch still loves the intrigue and excitement of being a traditional journalist as well and has no plans to leave that behind permanently. "At the moment I'm having too much fun straddling both worlds. Journalism and content marketing fulfill me in slightly different ways," he says. "Part of what I enjoy about content marketing is that it's solid, reliable, steady work. I go to bed at night and I know what I have to tackle the next day. I can plan. And that's marvellous."

On the other hand, he says, "Part of what I love about journalism is that suddenly it can tip your whole world on its head and you can end up at the center of something really exciting, in incredible places, talking to amazing people."

"Recently, for instance, I found myself in the Netherlands covering the MH17 disaster," Hatch says. "When I woke that morning, I had no idea that I'd be in Amsterdam by lunchtime—or that I'd spend the next week covering what was the biggest story in the world at the time."

The draw to journalism isn't just all about the glamour and adventure. "Also, from a 'personal brand' perspective, my ongoing role as a journalist gives a kind of weight to my content marketing work. I can 'leverage' it, if you like."

If the lack of storytelling talent in so many marketing departments is any measure, there are plenty of journalists out there still hesitating to cross over and put their skills to use in the name of brand journalism. Hopefully, I've done my part toward persuading you, but Hatch has some down-to-earth advice of his own: "Don't knock it 'til you've tried it."

That doesn't mean he doesn't understand your hesitation. "I think there's a lot of snobbery in our profession. And I understand that. You work hard to get into it, it's cut-throat and opportunities are limited, it's much maligned by the public, you're often abused and hated, but at the end of the day you do an important job as a member of the Fourth Estate and you feel like you're doing something special," Hatch says. "So for many journos, writing content falls right in alongside all the other dark arts—like public relations and being a political media advisor."

Daniel Hatch's Content Marketing Stars

Hatch says, "Without question [my favorite recent example of content marketing] is the stuff Marks and Spencer has done with Anna Chancellor ('Duckface' from *Four Weddings and a Funeral*). You'd never know it was M&S content." (See Figure 6.3.)

He adds, "She's one of their models and they created some video content and articles which are on the lifestyle blog on their website. But you'd never know the articles/videos were produced by M&S—they talk about her, her acting, her role in *Four Weddings*, her home in Hastings."

It's not just the content itself that got his attention. "What's incredible is how much 'earned media' it has gained in places like

Figure 6.3 Marks and Spencer created engaging blog content around actress Anna Chancellor.

The Daily Mail and *The Mirror*. But I've seen it on the *Guardian* website!" he says. "Expertly timed, too, given she's about to join Downton Abbey."

Changing the Publishing Paradigm

The content marketing industry is in flux. Some may still be able to stumble into a career in brand journalism, but as it becomes a more established profession hiring managers will be looking for more specific skill sets. During my conversation with Crossfield, he stressed the importance of understanding how to use a content management system and even—perhaps—knowing a bit of coding or having some video editing skills. This makes you a more attractive prospect.

In my day job as an editor I am fond of saying, "You can teach someone about subject matter, but you can't teach them to write." In other words, the most important thing to me is that you know how to put together a good story. Any halfway decent journalist should be capable of researching a subject enough to form a basic understanding of it, but not everyone can then turn what they have learned into a compelling story. This is as important for a content marketer as it is for a reporter.

As a journalist, you should be one step ahead of your competition, thanks to your inherent storytelling skills. Publishers already know this and are using it to their advantage by setting up the in-house content studios I mentioned in earlier chapters. They have started making it easier for brands to create great content marketing by making the talented writers they already have on staff available to the brands who might otherwise be looking to hire them for their own in-house marketing departments.

Of course, many of the same ethical dilemmas and concerns that plague journalists about making the switch to content marketing bother publishers. That seems to be borne out by the statistics. A 2014 Cxense "Extraordinary Insight" survey of over 260 publishing executives revealed that just 20 percent of respondents were running native ads. Despite that low number, 25 percent planned to introduce native ads over the next year. That number is still relatively low considering the increasing importance of content marketing—and by extension—native advertising to brands.

Publishers need to stop hesitating. Many of the industry's biggest players—from the *New York Times* to Conde Nast—have already figured out that to stay relevant to their advertisers they need to offer content services. Hemming and hawing (with a heaping side of hand-wringing) over the ethics of these tactics won't do anyone any good if there is no newsroom left to worry about compromising.

Part III

Publishers and the Custom Content Boom

Chapter 7

The Publishing Game Has Changed, So Should You

Whether you're a publishing veteran or fresh out of college, chances are if you work in the media it no longer resembles the industry you thought you would be building a career in. Long-time editors are adjusting to a world where the dividing line between the editorial and business sides of publishing is vanishing. Bright-eyed 22-year-olds fresh out of university are realizing that the digital revolution did not necessarily lead to an abundance of new media jobs—and certainly not high-paying ones. No matter where you are on that spectrum, you can probably blame your audience for the changes you see around you. As consumers become less and less willing to pay for content, publishers become more and more reliant on ad revenue—and have to implement all the changes you are seeing (and maybe lamenting).

Despite what has seemed like eternal doom and gloom in the news industry, the business is not on its last legs—at least not as a whole. In its report, *State of the News Media 2014,* Pew Research's Journalism Project found plenty of reason to be bullish. "Digital players have exploded onto the news scene, bringing technological know-how and new money and luring top talent," Amy Mitchell wrote in the report's overview. She pointed to the fact that BuzzFeed "once scoffed at for content viewed as 'click bait,' now has a news staff of 170, including top names like Pulitzer Prize-winner Mark Schoofs, and is the kind of place that ProPublica's Paul Steiger says he would want to work at if he were young again."

Investments from the likes of Jeff Bezos, John Henry, and Pierre Omidyar also have Pew praising the current state of the news media. But no matter where you turn in the Pew report one thing seems clear: Technology and a profound understanding of how it works is key to success in the new media landscape. Mitchell writes that many of the successful digital brands are "built around an innate understanding of technology" and that those important investors "are tech industry insiders and news media outsiders."

Curation and Licensing to Publishers' Rescue?

"Traditional ad revenue is declining as a result in consumer behavioral changes set in motion by the rise of social media, the demands of the savvy user and the fragmentation of the reading experience. Content marketing is a response, by advertisers, to these changing patterns in consumption. It is an effort to continue to reach their desired audience where, and in the way, these readers want to be reached. Adopting content marketing as a growing need of brands' is critical to any publisher dependent on advertising for revenue.

"NewsCred can help publishers earn revenue by licensing their content to these brands with zero lifting on their part and having direct relationships with the brands themselves. NewsCred mostly works directly with brands, as opposed to agencies, and we are building long term relationships that, unlike ad campaigns, are always on. Over the past year, NewsCred has been laying the foundation for content marketing success and educating brands on how to execute and what works. Licensed content was one pillar of the entry level strategy. This next phase will be about deepening those relationships and NewsCred will be unveiling some new ways for our publishers and brands to work together more collaboratively in our platform."

Jennifer Stenger, Director of Publisher Development, NewsCred

Perhaps the most important insight from the Pew report is the acknowledgment that social media and the news media would, frankly, be lost without each other. Mitchell writes, "The year also brought more evidence than ever that news is a part of the explosion of social media and mobile devices, and in a way that could offer opportunity to reach more people with news than ever before. Half of Facebook users get news there even though they did not go there looking for it. And the Facebook users who get news at the highest rates are 18-to-29-year-olds." It's clear that social networks are key to news and media outlets distributing their content and salvaging what little brand loyalty remains among their younger readers.

While the pessimism of years past may seem to have eroded a bit, it's important to look deeper at the numbers. Mitchell writes that "Our first-ever accounting found roughly 5,000 full-time professional jobs at nearly 500 digital news outlets, most of which were created in the past half dozen years. But the vast majority of bodies producing original reporting still comes from the newspaper industry. But those newspaper jobs are far from secure. Full-time professional newsroom employment declined another 6.4 percent in 2012 with more losses expected for 2013."

What does all of this mean to the average joe just getting out of college and looking for a job in the news media? Well, you're a lot more likely to find a job rehashing news you saw elsewhere on the web than you are to find a gig where you can do valuable, original reporting. Think about the sites you read every day. Sure, you might stop by the *New York Times*, NPR, or the *Wall Street Journal*, but you probably also visit Gawker and BuzzFeed. Sites like this do some original reporting and plenty of opinion pieces, but they do a whole lot more curation. Quite often, they are just summing up an article that originally appeared elsewhere and then, maybe, adding their own (often snarky) spin on the subject.

If you're a veteran journalist toiling away in a newsroom somewhere, you may want to keep an eye out for the man with the pink slip. And, if you're the publisher, you're in a very tough spot—trying to find a balance between keeping your advertisers happy (and your lights on), maintaining your audience's trust, and keeping your journalists happy.

Yes, the game is changing and, more and more, the likely winners seem to be those who are willing to embrace change and technology to reimagine the user experience and provide new value to the advertisers who are propping up the industry. Of course, technology isn't the only answer to the publishing world's dilemmas—as some publishers are finding out first hand.

Confronting Digital Reality at the *New Republic*

All hell broke loose at the *New Republic* (*TNR*) in December 2014. It was almost comical—as long as you weren't actually working there. The magazine experienced a mass (and very public) exodus of editorial staff, complete with an open letter published on Robert Reich's Facebook page. Here is the gist of the letter: "The magazine's present owner and managers claim they are giving it new relevance while remaining true to its century-old mission.... The New Republic cannot be merely a 'brand.' It has never been and cannot be a 'media company' that markets 'content.'... It is not, or not primarily, a business. It is a voice, even a cause. It has lasted through numerous transformations of the 'media landscape'—transformations that, far from rendering its work obsolete, have made that work ever more valuable."

The "present owner" is Chris Hughes, co-founder of Facebook. He took to the *Washington Post* to explain his side of the story. Hughes wrote, "If we wanted to chase traffic with listicles and slide shows, we would have. Instead, I have spent the last two and a half years supporting an institution whose mission I believe in and investing millions of dollars into its singular journalism so that it can continue to be influential and important."

Hughes' plans, according to *TNR*'s CEO Guy Vidra, include turning the magazine into a "vertically integrated digital product." That level of jargon-y nonsense is enough to scare anyone right out the front door. However, even the crankiest, dustiest corners of my journalist's soul think the folks at *TNR* are overreacting.

This isn't about old media versus new media. This is about reality, something the open letter on Facebook seems a bit out of touch with. It concludes, "It is a sad irony that at this perilous moment, with a reactionary variant of conservatism in the ascendancy, liberalism's central journal should be scuttled with flagrant and frivolous abandon. The promise of American life has been dealt a lamentable blow."

A tad dramatic, don't you think? *The New Yorker* says no. George Packer writes, "I highly doubt that Hughes wanted this debacle. He didn't plan for a change at the top to expose the emptiness of his commitment to the hard work of journalism." But did it? Or did the staff members reveal its complete unwillingness to confront reality and make the necessary changes to ensure its beloved publication continues to be viable?

On *TNR*'s site Vidra wrote, in his own open letter, "Over the coming months we will add to our masthead and bring on a great and diverse set of writers and editors. We will also invest in product managers, engineers, designers, data visualization and multimedia editors. We will build a platform that lets us create unique and compelling experiences on our web site and on mobile platforms, as well as the means to reach audiences outside our walls."

Most journalists confronted the new reality of the digital world a long time ago. I would have thought that, by now, editors would understand that becoming a viable digital property doesn't mean becoming BuzzFeed. It doesn't have to mean listicles and slideshows of cat gifs. That being said, it's hard to know what is actually going on inside *TNR*. It's even harder to know what general statements (such as this one from Vidra, "What will not change is our dedication to the ideals that underpin our institution—experimentation, opinion, argument, ideas, and quality") mean until the new strategies are implemented. Who knows—maybe the next time you head over to *TNR* looking for a takedown of Senator Mitch

McConnell, you'll find a tiny hamster eating a burrito instead. But I wouldn't bet on it.

I would be on the lookout for new mobile products, more multimedia experiences, and content—excuse me—*journalism* that is more targeted and personalized. For many hallowed journalistic institutions, these techniques are already part of daily business.

"The New Republic is a kind of public trust. That is something all its previous owners and publishers understood and respected. The legacy has now been trashed, the trust violated." That's what the former *TNR* editors say, but it sounds to me as if they are lamenting the changing face of journalism—not just their own magazine. For too long, journalists have been removed from the business side of the industry—as they get smacked with that reality, tantrums will ensue, but it doesn't have to be the end.

The Revenue Stream

According to Pew's research, the American news industry rakes in somewhere between $63 billion and $65 billion in annual revenue. (Those aren't exactly Walmart numbers but it's still nothing to scoff at!) Only 24 percent of that comes from subscribers while 69 percent of the revenue comes from advertisers. Advertisers who are, increasingly, demanding more bang for their buck have made it clear that boring old banners won't cut it anymore. No, they want to provide engaging content to your audience that is on par with the quality content you provide every day. They want to use your platform to get their message across—and they may even want to use your staff to create that content.

Mitchell and Jesse Holcomb looked at the Pew report's finding in "The Revenue Picture for American Journalism and How It Is Changing." They wrote, "Digital advertising is growing, though not nearly fast enough to keep pace with declines in legacy ad formats.

And, while new forms of digital advertising gained momentum in 2013, the online advertising market seems to favor a scale achievable only by few."

Did you catch that reference to "new forms of digital advertising?" What could Pew possibly mean by that? I think it's clear. Native advertising and content marketing are starting to play a bigger role in publishers' bottom lines.

In 2014, Digital Content Next found that 73 percent of its members currently offered native advertising solutions to advertisers. Yet, the Cxense "Extraordinary Insight" survey found that just 20 percent of respondents were running native ads. Clearly there's a big gap between the premium brands that make up the DCN membership (think ESPN and NBC Universal) and the rest of the media world—and that's a crying shame. Small niche and trade publishers have plenty to offer when it comes to creating native advertising. Your audience may not be as big as the big guys', but it is almost certainly more targeted. So before your advertisers have a chance to poach your writers to become in-house content marketers for them, it may be time to start thinking about building your own in-house team to cater to the content marketing demands of your advertisers.

There is no time like the present for publishers to finally hop on the content marketing bandwagon. As Joe Pulizzi told Lin Pophal for "The State of Content Marketing" in the January/February 2015 issue of *EContent*, brands are ready to start paying to promote their content: "Pulizzi feels there will be a shift from continuing to create new content in 2015 to strategically considering how to best deploy existing content. 'We are expecting a bigger move into paid content promotion in 2015,' he says. 'So many brands are creating loads of content that is going ignored. I believe, in many cases, some brands will pull back on creation and put more dollars behind the content they are currently creating or their core content for key audiences.' Another Pulizzi prediction is, 'I believe we will start seeing a large M&A [mergers and acquisitions] movement within enterprises, where many large companies will start to buy niche media companies where there is a gap in content and/or audience.'"

EContent: *What advice do you have for publishers who are worried about the impact content marketing might have on their advertising revenues?*

Joe Pulizzi: A couple things. First, publishers better invest in your content product so that it's best in class. Their advertisers are out there right now trying to grab all the attention with their own content. The publishers' audience has to be better than that of advertisers.

Second, publishers need to make a decision whether or not they are going to help advertisers create better content. There is a revenue opportunity there to assist in advertiser content creation, but it needs to be a focused effort in order to work (lots of competition there).

Third, prepare for a replacement now to advertising programs, like display advertising, that doesn't perform. I'd start making the switch to sponsorship models and event sponsorship, where there is more of a barrier to entry. Long story short, most brands have way more resources than publishers do, but that doesn't mean that publishers can't be better at the craft. Stay focused.

Excerpted from "Q&A: Joe Pulizzi, Founder, Content Marketing Institute" (EContentmag.com)

Custom Content

B2B publishers are no strangers to custom content. Companies like Reed-Elsevier and Penton have entire custom content wings. In fact, Penton is where Joe Pulizzi got his start. What might be a bit confusing for publishers who have been creating custom content for years—even decades—is just what the heck the difference is between it and content marketing.

Good question!

Over at CMI, Joe Pulizzi says there isn't really a difference. "Today, custom publishing is used mostly as the term and process for outsourcing the process of content marketing," Pulizzi wrote in

"Custom Publishing vs. Content Marketing." That seems like a pretty reasonable definition, though not everyone is on board with that analysis.

Andrew Boer tackled the topic on the Adotas site in a post titled (what else?) "The Difference Between Content Marketing and Custom Content." He wrote, "Custom Content is the creation of 'branded content' for a customer. And, for the most part, custom content is created for the client to communicate with their own existing customers." As for content marketing, Boer wrote that "Content Marketing is predominantly outward facing—it is about creating content that will attract *new* customers for brands. It can be branded content, but it can also be simply 'brand-relevant' content that attracts an audience."

After reading this, one may ask, "So, then what's the difference between custom content and native advertising?"

That is the million dollar question!

And the answer is, well, "not much." I don't necessarily agree with Boer that custom content is aimed at existing customers, or that content marketing is always for the benefit of new customers. I tend to agree with Pulizzi that the real difference lies in who is creating the content.

According to Pullizi, "The reason why custom publishing was adopted as the preferred term was because it was created by (wait for it), publishers. Without knowing what to call it, these (mostly magazine publishers) called it customized publishing. They needed to differentiate that business (creating assets not for the media company but for advertisers) from their core business. From the start, custom publishing was the wrong name…because publishing is not necessarily marketing…and creating content to sell products and services is all about marketing."

If custom publishing is, as Pulizzi says, just what you call it when a brand pays a publisher to create its content marketing, well, then it's basically native advertising right? I suppose there may be one difference. A publisher might create a piece of custom content for a client for a fee, and that client could go post it on their own blog or shop it around elsewhere. Native advertising is created to look like the publisher's own content and, therefore, must be distributed through the publisher's platforms.

What I'm getting at here is that even publishers have been in the content marketing game for longer than they realize. Continuing to play coy and turn the company nose up at native advertising is silly—and counterproductive to your goal of staying in business.

The Millennial Motivation

Capturing anyone's attention on the web isn't easy these days, let alone the sought-after attention of millennials. But native advertising may be just the right fit for this constantly distracted audience. According to *Content Marketing: Best Practices Among Millennials* from Yahoo!, Tumblr, Razorfish, and Digitas, 76 percent of millennials want to be informed on specific subjects while 75 percent "want to learn things and become smarter." More specifically, 45 percent are looking for resources to help them through a financial crisis. It's clear that content marketing and native advertising has the ability to reach digital natives. The report bears this out, saying that 46 percent of millennials who notice branded content on Yahoo consume it, and one third of those share it. See Figure 7.1 for more information from the report.

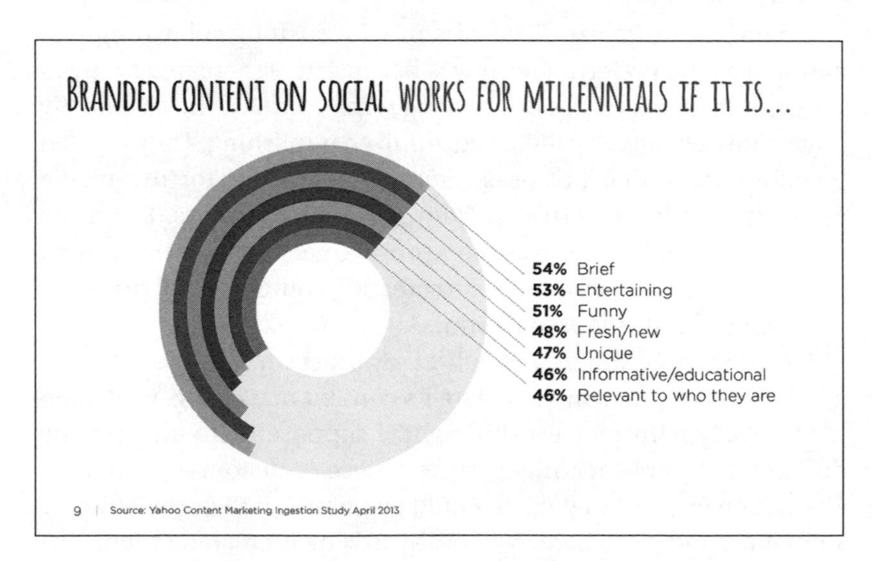

Figure 7.1 A chart from Yahoo's Content Marketing Ingestion Study outlines what kind of branded content works for millennials.

Don't Blame Your Audience

Audience trust is important; there is no disputing that. But if you're a publisher still clinging to the idea that getting into custom content—or native advertising—will compromise your audience's trust, you're wrong. It's not about whether or not you hop on the bandwagon; it's about how you implement your strategy.

According to the Custom Content Council, "A new study—'Consumers' Attitudes Toward Custom Content'—shows that seven in 10 consumers say they like custom content because it is tailored to their specific interests." Here is the thing: This study isn't new anymore. It was from 2011. If you're still resisting custom content, you're already years behind your customers. The Custom Content Council continues, "More than three-quarters say they understand that these companies are selling something, but feel it is okay since the information provided is valuable. Seven in 10 consumers say they prefer to learn about a company through a collection of articles rather than in an ad."

Readers may be embracing custom content, but that doesn't mean they aren't concerned about the state of journalism ethics. Civic Science put out a report called "Insight Report: Can the News Be Saved? Consumer Sentiment on Funding Objective Journalism" in early 2015. The research found "48 percent of respondents say they are 'very concerned' about the issue of preserving objective journalism, with about 76 percent claiming to be at least somewhat concerned." That, however, does not mean people are willing to pony up the dollars to keep their news "unbiased." Civic Science says, "When consumers are asked to select the best option for funding objective journalism, advertising sales leads with 47 percent of responses, followed by public financing (20%), charitable donations (18%), and requiring payment to access content (15%)."

The research from Civic Science may give some publishers pause. This seems like it should go without saying, but, perhaps, no one has put it plainly: Brands would not be so gung-ho about creating content marketing and native advertising if their customers didn't want it. In this love triangle, publishers seem to be the only holdouts. That being said, implementation is key.

"Think about it: Winning your customer's trust is challenging, but essential. It takes time and effort. Like all valuable relationships, it is not something to be trifled with for short-term gain," wrote Michelle Manafy in her Inc. column, "Trust Me: Content Marketing Is Risky Business." She continued, "Believe me, most media companies—like most other businesses—must take customer relationships seriously if they hope to survive."

Luckily, getting into the native advertising business doesn't have to compromise the hard-won trust you've established with your audience. Manafy continued, "One of the most difficult components of native advertising…is transparency. [Digital Content Next] research revealed that clear labeling is an essential component of successful native advertising endeavors."

The gist: As long as you're honest and transparent with your audience they will actually appreciate your native advertising endeavors. Would you rather have a banner pop up every time you go to a site, one of those annoying ads that suddenly starts playing a video extolling the benefits of Product X, or a well-crafted piece of content that reels you in with its quality? If the latter option sounds preferable to you, it probably sounds best to your audience as well.

Some companies are still learning this lesson, adjusting as they go.

American Express Modifies Native Advertising Practices

American Express, which operates the OPENForum.com website, has informed the National Advertising Division (NAD) that it has modified its native advertising practices to assure that consumers who click on OPENForum images-plus-text "ad units" are aware that the content is sponsored by American Express.

NAD, an investigative unit of the advertising industry's system of self-regulation, examines advertising claims in all mediums for truth and accuracy. American Express maintains "OPENForum" where it shares information designed for small-business owners and offers links to other American Express cards and services. American Express advertises the OPENForum site elsewhere on the internet through the use of content "recommendation widgets" from Taboola, Inc.

In its initial review, NAD was concerned that the links to OPENForum placed in Taboola recommendation widgets could be understood by consumers to mean that they were being directed to independent editorial content rather than sponsored content. The links consisted of a small picture, the title of the article, and the link's label, which read "OPEN Forum."

American Express, in response to NAD's inquiry, explained that "OPEN" is a brand geared to small-business owners, that the OPEN brand was clearly labeled on the links, and that the links brought users to the OPENForum site for articles containing advice for small-business owners. American Express further advised NAD that its labeling of links to articles on its OPENForum website had been permanently modified, and such links are now labeled as either presented by "American Express OPEN" or "American Express OPEN Forum."

The advertiser further noted that Taboola has, in the past year, begun the process of changing the "by Taboola" credit line to more clearly and conspicuously identify its links as sponsored.

NAD says it appreciated that American Express voluntarily made changes to the label on links to its OPEN Forum website, and that the changes provided greater transparency to consumers regarding the website to which consumers would be directed, an action NAD deemed necessary and appropriate.

EContentmag.com

Luckily, you no longer have to learn on the fly. There are enough publishers out there already offering custom content and native advertising that there are plenty of examples to learn from, good *and* bad.

In "The *Wall Street Journal*'s guide to making great native ads" on Digiday, Brian Braiker pulled together a list of guidelines based on advice from Trevor Fellows at WSJ Custom Studios. For Fellows, native success requires you to

- Get aligned
- Act quickly
- Make it interesting
- Amplify
- Measure, measure, measure

While transparency is notably missing from this list, that may be because it should go without saying. Sometimes though, it isn't just about putting a "Sponsored By" tag at the top. Some publishers have gotten into hot water with readers by not thinking through their partnerships and failing to live up to ethical expectations.

When Native Advertising Goes Wrong

I firmly believe that native advertising—or custom content, or branded journalism—has a place in the publishing business, but that does not mean everyone gets it right all of the time. Many companies are learning as they go and mistakes are made—both big and small. While sites like BuzzFeed (which was at one time known mostly for silly quizzes and cat gifs) may not have much to lose by embracing native advertising, more established and respected publications like the *New York Times* and the *Atlantic* have come under fire for their content missteps.

While the *New York Times'* promotion of *Orange Is the New Black* may be one of the best examples of native advertising, some of its other content has raised a few eyebrows, including those of John Oliver (see Figure 7.2). In the case of a native advertising partnership with Chevron (see Figure 7.3), the problem was not transparency.

Figure 7.2 A still from *This Week Tonight with John Oliver* criticizing branded content.

SECTIONS HOME SEARCH

The New York Times

TBrandStudio

How Our Energy Needs Are Changing, In A Series Of Interactive Charts

More so than ever before, the United States is powered by a diverse mix of energy sources. The interactive diagrams that follow explore the past, present and future of this complex system. The first maps out the composition of our primary sources of energy — from crude oil to solar power — and their different uses. The second visualization explains how those energy sources have diversified since the 1700s. The final diagram shifts to a global view, to show how — despite growing domestic energy production — rising demand overseas is intensifying competition for all types of energy.

Written and Produced by
TBrandStudio

What Kinds Of Energy We Use And What We Use It For

When Key Energy Sources Entered The Mix And How They've Evolved

Where Global Demand Is Highest And How It Will Grow

Figure 7.3 A screenshot from T Brand Studio's article for Chevron.

The article was just as clearly marked as any other native ad on the *Times* site. The problem was the client. Creating custom content can be tricky when the client is in a controversial industry. It's probably pretty clear to the folks at *Organic Gardening* magazine or *Mother Jones* that creating a native ad for an oil company would cross a line, but it's harder for a more general interest news outlet like the *New York Times*. The charts and numbers presented in the Chevron piece may have been accurate, but it's safe to say that if a reporter had set out to independently report the same topic there would have been a lot more to the story.

While the outcry over this incident didn't reach the level of the *Atlantic* Scientology debacle, it *did* draw the attention of some and serves as a great illustration of just how tough it can be to tread the fine line of trust when it comes to native advertising.

Of course, most publishers won't ever find themselves trying to decide whether branded content from controversial companies is right for them. Trade and niche publishers know their audiences better than anyone and have a limited pool of relevant advertisers to draw from.

Take *EContent,* for instance. It's unlikely we will ever be faced with deciding whether or not to create an ad for the likes of Exxon, Monsanto, or Walmart. Instead, *EContent* can create custom or branded content for the same CMS providers, marketing automation companies, and social media monitoring tools that might buy traditional ad space in its pages or that are already running white papers across channels. This simplifies our task as publishers in the era of branded content, and—at least in this one way—the big guys are at a bit of a disadvantage. Sure they have more and bigger advertisers to draw from, but they also have more rope to hang themselves with.

The road to becoming a custom content creator may be fraught with peril, but plenty of companies have already walked it. Learn from their mistakes, and plan meticulously to create your own content studio that will benefit your audience, your advertisers, and your bottom line.

Chapter 8

Become a Custom Content Creator

Starting your own custom content wing may sound daunting, but as a publisher you already have the basic building blocks in place: content creators, the tools they use—from basic word processors to video equipment—and a distribution network. What matters here is that you have access to content-building talent and know-how.

In his post "Creating a Custom Content Project? Here's Your Four Options," Joe Pulizzi of the Content Marketing Institute (CMI) advises marketers to hire a custom content publisher and not to go it alone if they don't have to. Why? Because, he writes, "Content creation and execution, especially from an integrated standpoint where print, online and in-person integration are involved, can be extremely complex. Also, in many cases, it's actually less expensive to outsource." With a built-in staff (and existing stable of freelancers), publishers—even those that have not been

Branded Content Gains Acceptance

"A new study by Vibrant shows that only 2 percent more of consumers trust content from publications (35%) than from brands (33%); and yet, there are more consumers who distrust content from publications (18%) than there are who distrust content from brands (15.5%). Additionally, the number of consumers that distrust content from media titles they know (12%) is double the number who distrust content from brands that they know (6%)."

Erik J. Martin, "In Branded Content We Trust" (EContentmag.com)

in the custom content business in the past—can be ready to create relevant materials at a moment's notice.

A study by Chartbeat and the *New York Times* found "that most Paid Post content produced by T Brand Studio during the research period proved to be significantly more engaging than the content supplied by third parties." In other words, research confirms that content created by the *New York Times'* staff out-performed content provided by brands. Chartbeat looked at the number of unique visitors, the amount of active, engaged time on a page, and visits from search. T Brand Studio out-performed brand content in all of those categories: "Specifically, T Brand Studio-produced content generated 361 percent more unique visitors and 526 percent more time spent than advertiser-produced content."

The study also turned up some surprises in the results: "The research also shows that while traffic on median-performing Paid Posts does not outperform traffic on median-performing NYTimes.com editorial content, some high-performing T Brand Studio posts received enough traffic to generate as much engagement as some editorial content on NYTimes.com."

Yes, you read that right! The best of the branded content was just as popular as the *New York Times'* editorial content.

Your editorial team may be ready to crank out content for customers, but every new business endeavor needs a plan. In this chapter we will explore the routes to custom publishing success and how you can turn your content expertise into revenue.

Start Small

Deanna Zammit is the director at Digiday's Content Studio, and her first word of advice to anyone looking to get into the custom content business is to keep it simple. "Start small," she says. "Make sure you have someone with a journalism background who knows how to write content that is in keeping with your own voice, who understands your brand and your audience."

Even now, several years into Digiday's branded content effort, Zammit says she is careful not to take on more work than her team can handle at any one time and deliver up to the high standards she has set. But the Digiday team is always working on multiple projects at the same time to make sure there is a constant flow of branded content. "If a client wanted to own the entire website for a month, I would think that would be more of an investment than clients would want to make. But hey, make me an offer," Zammit says.

But how do you get started on that very first project or figure out what to offer customers? "I would take inventory of your content and identify two to three ongoing features that you do really well (ideally something that's not hard news)," says Dani Fankhauser, branded content editor at Bustle (formerly of Mashable). "Then think about how these can become ad products. At Bustle we did a whiteboard story where we'd ask women a question and take their picture with their answer written on the whiteboard. This was easy to swap in a theme relevant to a brand as part of a program. At Mashable, we had a photo challenge our community team did each week, but we could sell a version of it with brand integration. We knew our readers loved these types of articles so it was a win for both sides. Once you start selling branded content, you can do more customization, but starting with what you do best is a good proof of concept."

Keeping your content simple may be important in the beginning, but there are still lessons to be learned from more ambitious content endeavors. McMurry/TMG is a self-described "world leading marketing communications & content marketing consulting firm…" which lists print and digital publishing under its many offerings. "When I applied in January 2010 for a managing editor job at what was then known as TMG (formerly The Magazine Group), the only thing that stood out in the ad was that the names of the magazine and publisher weren't mentioned," says Marla Clark, former executive content editor at McMurry/TMG. "I knew that the position supported a technology magazine serving the education market and that TMG at the time called itself a custom publisher, but it wasn't until my interview that I discovered that I would be part of a large editorial team creating custom content for one of TMG's largest clients. Up to that point, I had never worked in an agency environment, where you're producing content that not only serves your readers but also the business interests of the client."

Clark is now vice president and editorial director at Imagination, a content marketing agency based in Chicago. "At McMurry/TMG, I was in the weeds of daily content creation as an editor, responsible for conceiving, assigning, editing and producing a quarterly print magazine for technology professionals in the K–12 market, as well as other content that served the client's business needs (including videos, webinars and white papers)," she says. "I wrote and edited copy every day, and it was my job to learn and track what was happening in educational technology and then develop stories that helped people using technology in schools do their jobs better."

In this case, McMurry/TMG is taking a page right out of Red Bull's playbook and creating an entire magazine for its client. But if you're just getting started in the custom content game, you'll want to set your sights a bit lower. Creating a whole magazine—complete with print distribution—is an expensive and time-consuming endeavor. It's a far cry from creating a white paper. In this case, it even requires a full-time editor for the project. With editorial staff at your disposal and established relationships with printers, it might be tempting to go big right out of the gate. *Don't!*

Start simple with something like those trusty old white papers, an engaging article, a series of short videos, or (if you're feeling adventurous) a short ebook. If you have the ability to conduct in-depth research of your audience, that is a great place to start. From there you can build the content around your results.

Nisha Gopalan, creative strategist and branded content manager at *New York Magazine,* has some added advice for publishers just starting down the branded content road. She says, "Set ambitious internal goals—both monetary and in metrics. Keep problem-solving until you meet those goals, then increase them. This keeps you honest."

Gopalan also suggests you keep tabs on the industry: "And read. Read what other branded content is out there. Read about new developments in content marketing. Read about social media; it's evolving every day.... And pitch to your strengths. The best competition comes from focusing on the branded-content you can do better than anyone else, and perfecting that. With that in mind, don't be afraid to take calculated risks in visuals or content. This is an area of growth; strive to be at the forefront of that."

Whatever happens, you do not want to over-promise in the beginning. Instead, keep the scope of your work small and the quality high. It's better to completely blow your client's socks off with a small project than to deliver mediocre work on a big one. Eventually, though, you may be able to work your way up to an entire magazine!

Make Someone Accountable

"In my current role at Imagination, I'm not an editor and I'm not working solely for one client. Instead, as the content director for new business programs, I spend my days conceiving and developing content programs for potential new clients. It's been fun and challenging to leverage my editorial skills in new ways," says Clark. "Instead of writing or editing stories that are then published in a print magazine, online or in some other format, I'm strategizing and fleshing out the what, why, and how of a content program for each new prospective client—and then presenting that framework and the creative work our designers and developers have executed in the hope of winning the business. I'm doing this kind of work for all types of companies in all types of industries, which means I'm always learning something new and tailoring content recommendations to the particular needs of the prospect and the audiences it serves."

One of the things I asserted early on in this book is that in order for a content marketing program to succeed it needs someone to be held accountable. Someone like Clark—or Zammit, or any of the other people I interviewed for *Inside Content Marketing*. As a publisher you may already have someone in your office ready to take on this responsibility—whether it's a writer, a marketer, or someone in your business department.

"Every stellar branded content editor I know has had [marketing and journalism experience], even if it's just a six-month copywriting internship, or vice versa. I wouldn't say the experience is necessary, but you do need to have an interest in learning the incentives and processes on both sides," says Fankhauser. "Typically you would be working with the sales team and the editorial team, essentially becoming the wall between the two, so it's best if you can empathize with both."

"I think it's more important to have a journalism background," says Zammit, though the ability to deal with clients is equally important. Among other things, she says, your branded content point person will have to "talk [the clients] around to your point of view and make them understand why your expertise is important."

Who you eventually choose for this all-important position will likely depend on how you plan on measuring success. If your new custom content wing is all about generating revenue, you will probably want someone who is more business-minded at the helm, but do not forget that great content is at the heart of your success.

Talking with Trendsetters: Deanna Zammit, Director, Digiday Content Studio

Having helped Digiday launch its Content Studio, Deanna Zammit knows what it takes to create a successful native advertising department. After starting her career in journalism—complete with a stint at *AdWeek*—and a turn at freelancing, Zammit happened to see a post on Facebook that announced Digiday was looking to find someone to head up its new Content Studio and said, "I can do that!"

While she was freelancing, Zammit started doing some work for J. Walter Thompson (JWT)—a 150-year-old marketing communications firm—as a sort of trends reporter. That work, combined with her experience at *AdWeek,* set her up for success in the hybrid world of brand journalism, where marketing and journalism collide. While her experience on the content side of things has been invaluable, there are still some parts of the business that Zammit is getting used to. When you're a reporter it's easy to ignore bad pitches, and tell off pesky PR flaks, but when you have clients, things change. "For clients you have to be responsive, you have to cater to their needs, you have to do something called education," says Zammit.

While a background in marketing might be necessary to help launch an entire branded content studio, Zammit says she looks for journalists when she's hiring. "The kind of storytelling you do through marketing and advertising is different from the kind of storytelling you do through journalism," she says. "I look for flexibility. I look for lack of ego...I look for someone who has business sensibility."

When you're writing from a marketing point of view, she says, your stories originate from questions like "What do we want to tell people, who do we want to be in front of people?" Zammit says, "For content marketing you have to start from the other point of view. What does the audience want? What is going to feed the audience's curiosity?"

Not just any reporter will do, however. "It's important to find journalists who have a particular sensibility," she says. "They need to understand business needs....You have to be able to see both sides of the coin and don't mind it.

"A lot of journalists go into journalism because they feel a burning passion for truth-telling," Zammit says. "It's wonderful and it's laudable....Certainly, as content marketers, we don't want to compromise that, but you also do have to thread in things like client services."

One of the ways to make those client interactions run more smoothly is to lay out ground rules for your clients. "We have a set of sponsored content guidelines that are pretty immutable," says Zammit. "One of our number one rules is that we don't discuss the client's products in the content we produce. The one exception is when the client is a consumer facing brand that we feel our audience would be interested in." The key to enforcing those guidelines is putting them in a contract.

"We get people who push back, and we try to push back in as gentle a way as possible," says Zammit. "We reach a compromise. We can't change a quote but maybe we can change this other line to be more palatable."

This is where the line between journalism and brand journalism "gets a little murky," as Zammit puts it. "Ultimately, at the end of the day, it is a marketing and advertising product and [the clients] are paying for it, but you want to hew as close as possible to what the real story is," she adds.

But as content marketing and native advertising gain steam, and become more a part of the mainstream, conflicts between editorial standards and client needs are few and far between, Zammit says. She jokes, "I haven't found someone in a while who wants to insert an executive quote."

Set Your Standards and Stick to Them

If you want to avoid compromising your audience's trust, you need to spend a lot of time laying out your standards for custom content—especially if it will ultimately be running alongside your own content. This may prove to be the hardest part of setting up your custom content operation.

If you're too loose with your standards, you risk losing your journalistic credibility—which is not only important to your audience but to your advertisers as well. After all, part of what they are paying for is the reputation you've built, but if you're too strict, you risk losing customers and valuable revenue. Take a look at Figure 8.1, taken from the webpage of Digiday's content studio.

It is clear from the moment a potential client visits the site that Digiday is not interested in creating self-serving, unethical, or dishonest content—not even for a fee. Of course, any client who understands content marketing will know that these kinds of standards are integral to success. "We always kind of knew what we wanted to do in terms of how we wanted it to look and feel, what the guidelines should be," Zammit says. "It took a while to codify those. I was new to client on-ramping. We needed to spell things out, put them in contracts, etc. We knew what the rules should be, we just didn't know we had to write them down."

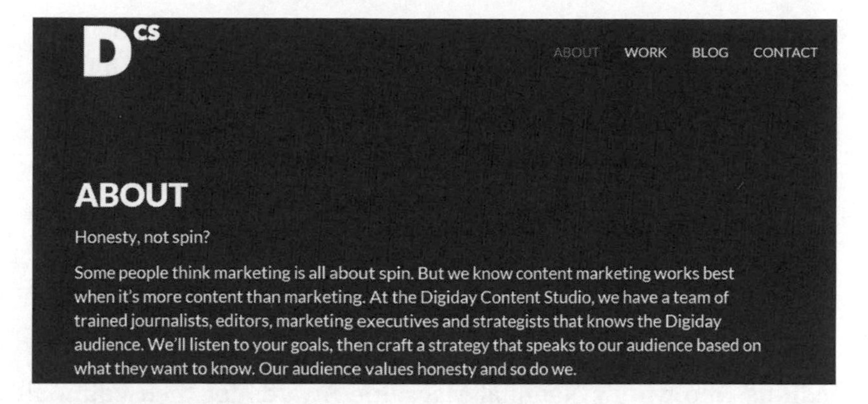

Figure 8.1 A screenshot from Digiday's Content Studio page, where the company lays out its philosophy in black and white.

Are you willing to create a not-technically-untrue piece of content for a company, even if it doesn't tell the whole story? How much input do the clients get? At what point do you decide to walk away from a potential client to preserve your audience's trust? These are questions you need to answer before you are confronted with them in a real-life situation.

Laying out the ground rules at the beginning of your relationship with a potential client takes the guess work out of your interactions. "Speaking specifically about native ad programs at publishers—we constantly work with the sales team to set expectations for clients," says Fankhauser. "A publication should have native ad products that are well-defined, but of course can be adjusted based on clients' needs. A lot of times the conversation is fluid, though—a brand will request something later in the process and we'll say, 'Hey, I think that will feel awkward to our readers, but let's do XYZ instead.'"

"Brands are often drawn towards hard sells like product mentions, which can feel forced, if it doesn't make sense in the content program that was sold. Balancing this with reader trust is mostly intuitive—if we see a strong topic with a good headline and visuals still not performing well in terms of traffic and shares, we might conclude something about how the branding was integrated is turning readers off," says Fankhauser.

She adds, "Ultimately this comes down to editorial judgment. Customers want their content to perform well, too, so we'll talk it through and strike a balance where we're able to experiment but still use our editorial expertise to ensure the brand isn't getting a negative impression with our readers."

"Our clients understand our playing field. In our case, there is a clear distinction between branded content and editorial content," says Gopalan. "The former is executed by our Creative Services team, the latter by several editorial writers and editors. Responsibilities do not overlap. *New York Magazine* has amazing writers and editors who win us National Magazine Awards for their editorial work. I think that gives us some clout, so clients respect that divide because it benefits them, too."

"Also, be sure to figure out your branded-content guidelines early on, such that your site has consistent verbiage and design throughout its branded content. If you're looking for a line of distinction between editorial and branded content, [The American Society of Magazine Editors'] suggestions can be very helpful. It's key for advertisers to know exactly what to expect," Gopalan adds.

What may be more complicated than simply laying guidelines is deciding when to turn a client away just because it isn't a fit for your publication. Zammit and Fankhauser assure me, however, that having to turn away clients is very unlikely.

"I can't imagine a situation where a company comes to us and we say, 'No we can't work with you'," says Zammit.

When I asked Fankhauser if she had ever turned away a potential client, she agreed with Zammit. "Never," she says. "If an advertiser wants to buy branded content, we'll work with them to put something together that will make everyone happy."

But what about the *Atlantic* and the infamous Scientology misstep? Surely someone should have spoken up and decided to turn down that particular client. No, say our experts.

"The goal of a publication's branded content is to create content that appeals to readers that is in line with a brand's values. This will be more difficult for some brands than others. Government and religious organizations, and pharmaceutical companies stand out because they can be more controversial, so the publication must get creative," says Fankhauser. "The problem arises when a brand wants content that is solely self-promotional, which readers rarely, if ever, respond well to. If Scientology had sponsored a series of Q&As with prominent non-Scientologists on how the pursuit of knowledge brings value to their lives, that might have been OK."

Gopalan adds, "Some advertisers will come to you aspirationally; others come to you because their brand would seem to already speak to your readership... Take time to internally determine what demographic they are seeking, and figure out how can that seamlessly overlap with your readership. Then craft your pitch thusly. Of course, some are going to be greater challenges than others."

To reiterate, having your guidelines and standards in place—and having a strong leader who can work with the brand to help them see the content marketing light—can go a long way toward heading off any problems with your clients (or your audience) before they even begin.

Remember: This Is *Brand* Journalism

Once you have your ducks in row, it's time to start thinking about execution. If you are turning to your staff writers and freelancers, they may need a reminder that creating custom content is different. "The biggest difference I found was that, in many cases, you're allowing your sources to review (and sometimes change) their contributions prior to publication," says Clark. "In traditional journalism, sources don't see their quotes or how the writer used the information they provided until the story has been published; the same is true for the writer, who typically doesn't see the edited piece until it's published. In custom publishing, the process is far more collaborative, with more back and forth between the writer and editor and between the writer/editor and sources."

Like most of the journalists-turned-content marketers I spoke to, Clark had an exceedingly realistic vision of journalism. She says, "Publishers often influence content, regardless of whether it's traditional or brand journalism. I've been fortunate to never work for one that made excessive or unseemly demands."

Your journalists may have trouble—at least initially—incorporating the "marketing" into content marketing. The process is still the same at its core. "Fundamentally, you're still doing the same thing—namely, trying to tell a good story. My process has been the same for every piece of content I've ever produced," says Clark. "In the early days of my career, I was responsible for one format—the print magazine. As the web took off, editors and writers had to start thinking about the digital experiencc, too, and how to repurpose print content for consumption online. That led to ancillary content and new formats such as slideshows, videos, checklists, blog and social media posts, and so on."

She continues, "Regardless of the content type, you have to start with research—studying the industry itself, the latest trends or news of note, the topic in question, the people involved. And then you have to use editorial judgment to distill the good information from the bad, the high-quality sources from the sketchy ones, the germane ideas that will resonate with readers from the irrelevant or wild-goose-chase ones that won't lead to anything new or interesting."

While the basics of good content don't change, Clark does acknowledge that there are some extra elements that brand journalists need to be aware of. She says, "In content marketing, unlike in most traditional journalism, you're trying to help your audience through a journey of some sort, which often ends with a purchase and new efforts to earn their loyalty. So you have to have a content strategy and regularly 'feed the beast' with fresh, quality content to keep your audiences engaged, to build their relationship with your brand, and to help them see and trust your brand as a useful source of information. If you don't have a master plan and a clear understanding of who your audiences are and why they need the information you're providing, you won't be successful in your storytelling."

In the second chapter of this book I offered a more detailed roadmap to great content marketing. Some of that will be useful here, though creating native advertising and custom content experiences is slightly different. On Clickz.com, a resource for marketing news and advice, Leah Block wrote "Native Advertising Litmus Test: 4 Questions To Ask of Your Content." She outlined the questions in her ClickZ article as follows:

Is your content meaningful and relevant to the consumer?
Content that is too promotional, broad, or irrelevant will cause consumers to look past it, just as they currently

look past banners. Instead of thinking like an advertiser as you build out your native advertising campaign, think like a publisher.

Is your content part of a larger story that can be extended and shared across other relevant channels? While one-off ideas may drive a quick spike in your performance, ongoing ideas will help build brand equity and performance over time. It will also help inspire future content.

Is your native advertising optimized for SEO so that it can be picked up by the search engines and drive more relevant, qualified traffic back to your brand (just like any PR piece, website, or landing page)?

Is your content being tested, analyzed and optimized like any other portion of an advertising campaign? Doing so allows for continued learning and improvements to your content, in order to better facilitate qualified, active engagement with your brand.

That last point is especially important for new custom content shops manned by former journalists. While there are some publishers that test, analyze, and optimize their content, most are driven by the news of their particular coverage area, and rely on the gut instincts of editors. When you have a client expecting results, that may not cut the mustard. But don't worry; the content marketing space is being flooded with tools, and there are some old stand-bys that may be effectively applied to your monitoring effort.

There are a lot of tools that can help you analyze your content after it's published, but one in particular—InboundWriter—caught my attention a couple years ago for promising to predict success before your content is even written. As CEO Skip Bestoff put it at the time, "Other analytics platforms might tell you whether BBQ, Bar-B-Q, or barbecue is the best keyword to use, but what we're answering is the higher-level question: 'Should I be writing about barbecue at all?'"

When InboundWriter went out of business late in 2015, its demise surprised me because that's exactly the kind of question

Content Marketing Tools to Keep Your Efforts on Track

As a publisher you're probably already tracking your analytics to some degree, but when clients get involved you have to be able to show your results. Just as importantly you have to be able to predict, with some measure of certainty, that the content you're creating for your customers will be a success. What follows is a short list of tools that can help you track your successes and failures; it is nowhere *near* comprehensive, and this is a moving target, so do your homework before settling on any one tool.

- **HubSpot**—When you need to eliminate the guesswork from content creation, HubSpot can help. It offers the ability to create and then monitor blogs posts, landing pages, and all the elements of your content marketing efforts. HubSpot is also a bit of a one-stop shop for your marketing efforts. You can schedule social media posts, and even get free white papers to help you brush up on your best practices.
- **BuzzSumo**—If your needs are a bit too modest to warrant a HubSpot subscription, then BuzzSumo might be more up your alley. This tool focuses on delivering analytics-driven insights. Use it to find the most shared articles in your niche, see who the key influencers are, and monitor your brand mentions.
- **Little Bird**—This company describes itself as an "influencer marketing platform" and says, "Volume metrics from listening platforms only tell part of the story. Make sure you focus your work on the strength of relationships." This tool helps you identify the people you need to engage with to boost your content and your social presence. Even seasoned professionals will want to have a look.
- **Skyword**—Skyword brands itself as the intersection between story and science and as a full content

marketing platform. It brings talent to the table as well as technology. Publishers looking to create a custom content wing might find Skyword to be overkill, but brands with an in-house team may find it to be just what the doctor ordered.

- **Google Analytics**—This free tool is probably already in your arsenal; don't hesitate to use it to get the lowdown on your branded content. It can tell you just about everything you need to know about your traffic and help you better understand what will drive results for your custom content clients.
- **Feedly**—Since Google closed its Reader application, Feedly has emerged as the heir apparent to the content curation throne. It can help marketers stay on top of the competition and find topic ideas.

content marketers and custom content creators need to ask themselves *before* writing blog posts, creating videos, and executing campaigns. Sadly, there may no longer be a tool dedicated to telling you whether your idea for an article is likely to score big with your audience, but if you cobble together enough tools and analysis, you just may be able to answer that question for yourself, save time, and deliver better results for your clients.

Build Relationships and a Process

Any good journalist knows that the relationships you build with your sources are integral to creating accurate, well-researched articles. In other words, "You're only as good as your sources." That's still true in brand journalism, but the relationships change a bit. Digiday understands that the partnership between the content studio and its clients is at the heart of great content.

David Amrani wrote "To Produce the Best Client Content, First Build Relationships" for Digiday's content studio website. He based much of the article on a talk given by Bill McGarry, executive director of digital advertising of the Hearst Men's Group, and Melissa Rosenthal, director of creative services at BuzzFeed, at a Content Marketing Breakfast event. Amrani writes, "BuzzFeed takes an active approach to client education with its BuzzFeed University, a formalized course that teaches sponsors about the process from a creative perspective." This is, obviously, an incredibly proactive approach to not only building client relationships but helping them understand the process, guidelines, and why it's all important to creating good content. Most publishers, however, aren't going to launch an entire client education program.

More often than not, your custom content team is going to start building relationships with clients as part of the content creation process. The simple act of asking questions—something journalists know how to do well—can get the ball rolling. This is when you get to know your clients and their goals, which is an important part of making content that keeps your customers coming back for more.

The "getting to know you" phase should be the beginning of your content creation process. Once you understand your client's goals, you can move on. Fankhauser says, "We first work with the brand to come up with a program and specific deliverables, like the total number of articles or infographics, events, videos or social contests. We might also send a list of topics or subjects (influencers) for the brand to approve. Other items we discuss could include a name for the program or a hashtag, if relevant."

At Digiday, Zammit says the process often begins with her pitching ideas to possible new clients. "Once the contract is signed we put them on our calendar and we do a kick-off call, learn about [the clients] and their goals," she says. Then the Content Studio team comes together to brainstorm possible ideas. Zammit says she models these brainstorming sessions after the weekly meetings she would partake in at *AdWeek*. She says the team asks, "What do we think will work? What are the client goals? What's in the news? What are the emerging trends?" From there they come up with a concept for a series, or video series, or a presentation at an event.

Fankhauser says that once the concept for the content is approved, "the branded content director or editor will assign out each piece, often to freelancers, unless they're lucky enough to have full time staff. The branded content team will then edit and ensure the content meets the brand's requirements before sending it on for approval, and once it's approved, it is scheduled to go live."

Zammit, however, warns that brands are not used to working as fast as journalists. When her team initially told brands they could turn around content within a week, she ran into a lot of push-back. "The publishing metabolism...doesn't always work for the client," she says. "Clients are used to planning way in advance...so publishers move a bit fast for them." Clients often need more time to review materials, and collect approvals, which has led the Digiday Content Studio to build in extra time to its production process.

Over at *New York Magazine*, "It starts with a brainstorm between me, the integrated marketing manager, the ad-sales person, and sometimes our creative director. We pitch that idea to the client," says Gopalan. "Once a campaign is sold through, if necessary, we book talent, host any photo or video shoots, and conduct interviews. Then we work with our writers and designers for the words and visuals, and—if the execution requires tech expertise—with our UX and dev team. Much of this is concurrent. Once we complete this process, we run it by the client for feedback."

She adds, "What's reassuring here is that at this stage in the process there can be a conversation. If they request a tweak that I don't understand the value of, I say something, and we discuss it. Sometimes they take our suggestions; other times they feel strongly enough about their feedback that we integrate it into the branded content. They realize we care, so it's viewed as helpful kick-back on our end. Ultimately, we only succeed if they do; we both want the same thing."

With your guidelines in place, a content director at the helm, and your process laid out in front of you, it's time to make great branded content. In the next chapter, we'll see what successful collaborations between publishers and brands look like.

Chapter 9

Branded Content in Action

One of the questions I asked everyone I interviewed for *Inside Content Marketing* was this: "What's your favorite piece of content marketing from the past year?" I received a variety of answers and have already detailed many of the examples in previous chapters. But when I spoke with brand journalists working at publishers, I asked them a similar but slightly different question. I wanted examples of their favorite branded content from their own websites. What they shared with me follows.

Dani Fankhauser, Branded Content Editor, Bustle

The branded content team at Bustle created "See What Inspires These 7 CEOs Each Morning" for L'Oreal. The slideshow consists of images of seven female CEOs in front of their mirrors, with an inspirational quote written in lipstick (the example in Figure 9.1 features Mariya Nurislamova, CEO of Scentbird).

Fankhauser says, "L'Oreal was a great brand to work with and brainstormed their stories with our team so we were able to come up with something very much in line with the brand's values, but performed incredibly well with Facebook traffic because the article featured interesting women who had large networks on their own." This content not only captures the values of L'Oreal but is also a natural fit with Bustle's lifestyle content geared toward women. It takes into consideration the brand, the publication, and the readers.

But outside of Bustle's pages, what is Fankhauser's favorite example of branded content? For that, she turns to the *New York Times*. This example, I have to admit, kind of blew me away as well. The *New York Times* teamed up with Google to create

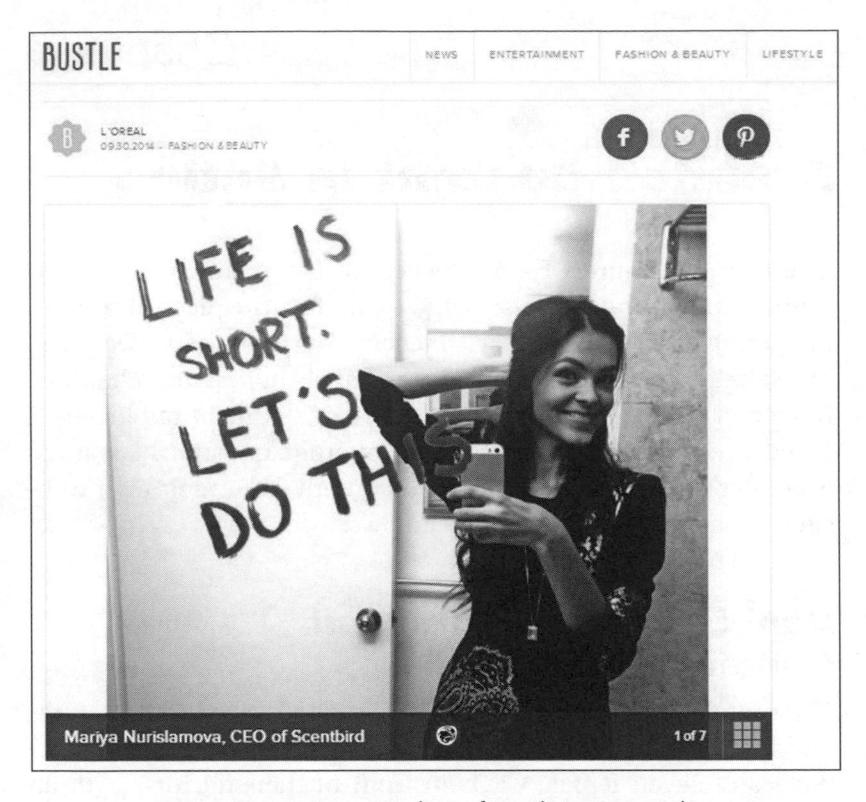

Figure 9.1 A screenshot of Bustle's "See What Inspires These 7 CEOs Each Morning" for L'Oreal.

something that goes beyond a mere branded post and creates an entire interactive experience that feels more like it's something cool that happens to be powered by Google than a plain ol' native ad.

On the "Plan Your Next Adventure with 36 Hours & Google Maps" page (Figure 9.2), readers find themselves with an interactive image of the earth in their browser window and Google's famous drop pins placed at a number of different cities. You can click on any place that strikes your interest, or hit the "Surprise Me" button to be taken to a mystery destination. Google then provides you with a complete itinerary for 36 hours spent in a given city—in the example in Figure 9.3, the city happens to be Copenhagen.

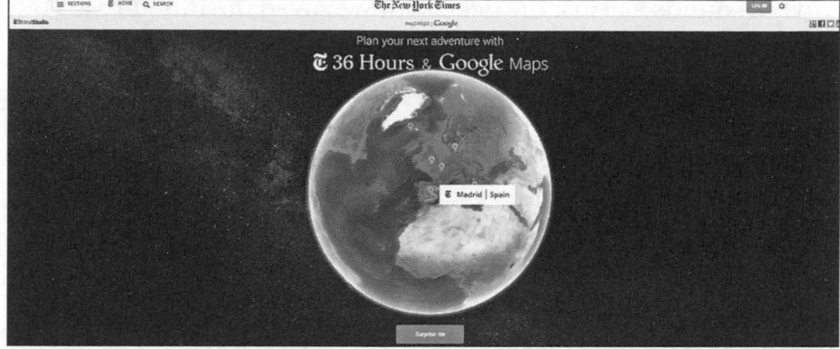

Figure 9.2 A screenshot of the *New York Times'* "Plan Your Next Adventure with 36 Hours & Google Maps."

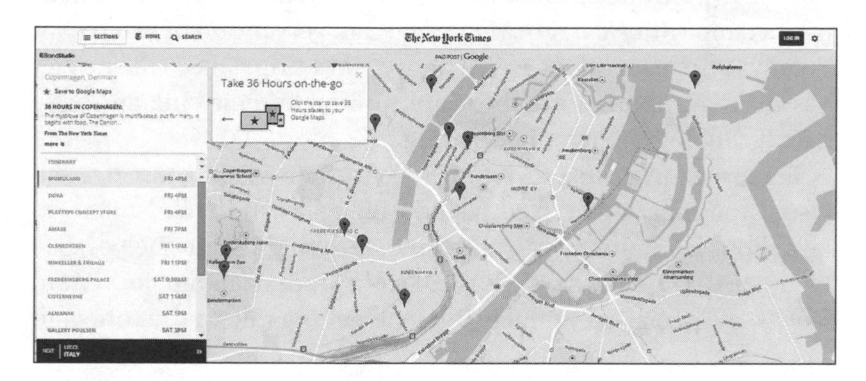

Figure 9.3 "Plan Your Next Adventure with 36 Hours & Google Maps" plotted out a 36-hour adventure in Copenhagen.

"There's a trend towards app-like experiences for branded content which I think allow for more brand integration than straight text content would, so I think we'll continue to see more interactive stuff like this," says Fankhauser. If a user actually gets inspired to visit one of the cities on the map—rather than just inspired to head over to Google.com—she can save the itinerary right to her Google account from the *New York Times'* page.

Imagine you're browsing the Travel section of *The Times.* Maybe you're thinking about taking a trip, but you don't have a destination in mind. You stumble across this post—which is, no doubt about it, an ad—and before you know it you've decided that 36 hours in

Madrid sounds like just the ticket! You've saved the itinerary to your Google account, and now you're using Google to search for flights.

This is exactly what can happen when a publisher knows its audience and a brand knows its own strengths. Everyone wins, including the consumer who just had one of the best, most helpful ad experiences of his life.

Nisha Gopalan, Creative Strategist and Branded Content Manager, *New York Magazine*

Is there any store more quintessentially New York than Tiffany & Co.? No, which makes the store the perfect fit for a branded content partnership with *New York Magazine.* "I'm very proud of two recent Tiffany & Co. executions we've done," says Gopalan. "The jeweler has really responded to our desire to mingle their chic aesthetic with technology, in a refined setting."

For "Fashion's Most Coveted: Style Insiders' Tiffany & Co. Wish Lists," the magazine asked fashion bloggers and trendsetters to talk about the items they wanted most from Tiffany's shelves (see Figure 9.4). Gopalan says, "Basically, we want branded content to feel like a special experience, but still feel organic to the tone and

Figure 9.4 A screenshot of *New York Magazine's* "Fashion's Most Coveted: Style Insiders' Tiffany & Co. Wish Lists."

aesthetic of the vertical you're reading—NYmag.com, Vulture, The Cut, Grubstreet, Science of Us, and so on. So whenever possible, we try to come up with ideas or experiences that possess an element of intrigue. Consuming branded content should be worth your time!"

In "Count Down to Your Most Exquisite Valentine's Day Ever" (see Figure 9.5), the magazine created an interactive calendar—sort of like an Advent calendar, only you get jewelry instead of candy—and then told readers to Tweet @NYFYI to get date and gift suggestions. You may notice that the examples from *New York Magazine* are heavier on brand and product integration than some of the examples we have already seen. Gopalan explains, "This was

Figure 9.5 A screenshot from "Count Down to Your Most Exquisite Valentine's Day Ever" by *New York Magazine*.

purely an aesthetic decision. The lighting and detail of photos Tiffany & Co. typically takes are spectacular; we knew this from experience. So why mess with perfection? We decided to take their photos and try something new with them—the magnifying effect—to show off that clarity. We knew this type of presentation, which is chic but interactive, would be something that would resonate with our readers."

The Humanitarian Giving Back Through Fashion

Sponsor story by

REVLON

STYLED BY THE CUT

Gel Envy by Revlon

Growing up in Guinea, Africa, Mariama Mounir Camara-Petrolawicz dreamed of coming to America to be an artist. Her affluent parents, however, wanted her to become a doctor. A rebellious teen, she left anyway—and did it on her own, with just $100 in her pocket. Today, Camara-Petrolawicz is a successful women's rights activist (through the There Is No Limit Foundation) and a textile designer (through Mariama Fashion Production). Her prints, created by African artisans, got a massive endorsement last year from Michelle Obama, who set off a tie-dye craze by donning a Tory Burch frock made of Camara-Petrolawicz's electric blue-on-white fabric.

"This is my passion. I needed to do something I loved," says the

Figure 9.6 A screenshot from "The Revlon Provocateurs" on *The Cut*.

Gopalan also pointed me toward "The Revlon Provocateurs" (see Figure 9.6 opposite) which appeared on *New York Magazine's* The Cut vertical. Like the Tiffany ads, this campaign focused on styling and then profiling interesting women. "We executed a five-month-long branded-content series for Revlon," she says. "The campaign really spoke to Revlon's imperative to celebrate smart, successful women whom the readers of The Cut could immediately relate to." This is a far more in-depth content-oriented native ad, which brings the stories of everyone from humanitarians to bloggers to The Cut's audience.

Beyond her own work, Gopalan says, "I'd have to high-five the *New York Times* Idea Lab for dedicating themselves to innovation. Every time they drop something new, it's a headline! And I'm definitely a fan of what *Forbes* does—terrific examples of elevating brands through smart reporting and sleek presentation."

Deanna Zammit, Director, Digiday Content Studio

Digiday's branded content extends beyond its website to its live events, which brings us to one of Zammit's favorite examples of her team's efforts. "For Xaxis, the premier sponsor at Digiday's Programmatic Summit, we attempted to reinvent the sizzle reel, producing a series of videos that dovetailed with the event content and felt at home on Digiday.com," (see Figure 9.7) according to a case study about the project. Zammit elaborates, "As Digiday is an

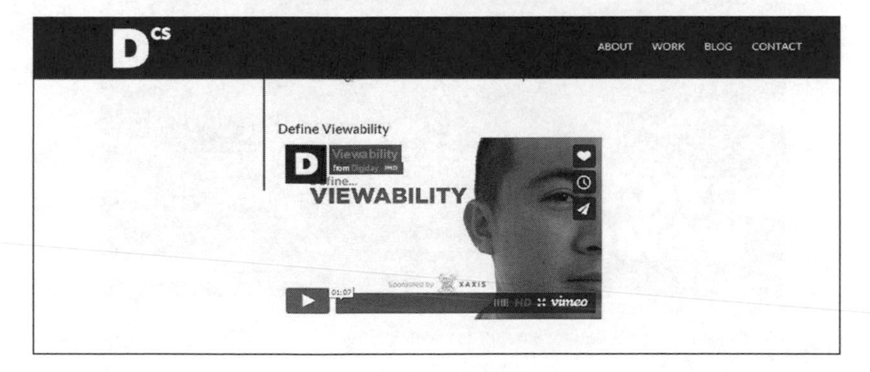

Figure 9.7 An example from Digiday's Content Studio of the videos it created for Xaxis and featured at Digiday's Programmatic Summit.

integrated platform, we used our Summit experience and publishing site to feature Xaxis as a sponsor of the debate around thorny issues like viewability and ad fraud. It was a truly native experience, featuring video interviews of event-specific speakers on topics that dove tailed with the Summit's editorial agenda."

The Xaxis videos are a great example of thinking outside the box to create content that benefits your clients as well as your audience, but on the more traditional branded content front Zammit points to a series of posts. "I'm also proud of our series for iStock by Getty Images—an article series that targeted advertising creatives at small agencies as well as freelancers who need cheap, high quality images to integrate into their work (see Figure 9.8). The series did especially well and showcased our ability to reach beyond ad tech clients and ad buying executives to the creative community. It also featured a mix of in-depth and lightweight, shareable content."

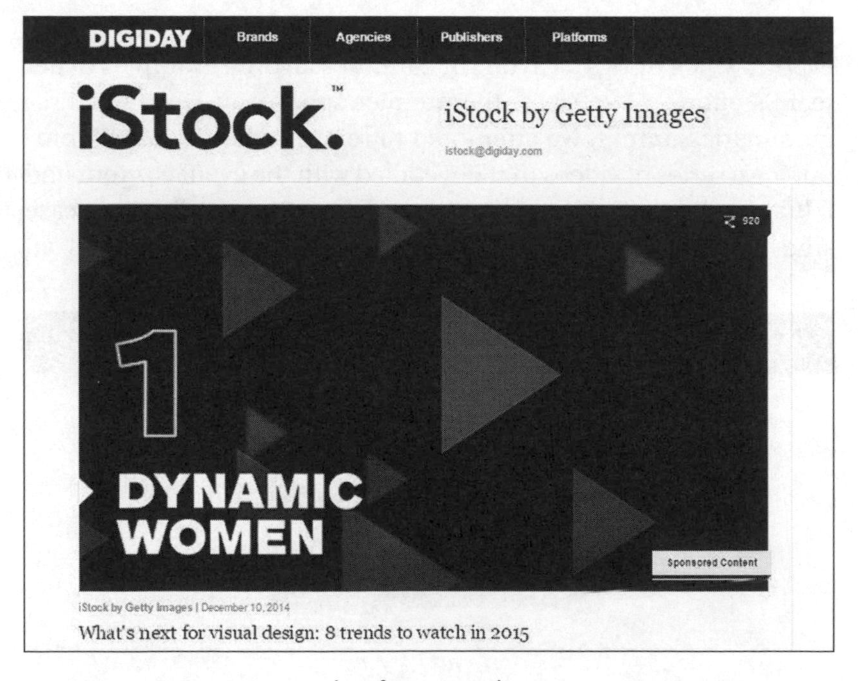

Figure 9.8 A screenshot from Digiday's campaign targeting advertising creatives for iStock by Getty Images.

The Best of Branded Content

The past few years have been big for branded content, and the business is only continuing to heat up. You can Google your way to countless "best of" lists, but I'll save you the trouble and detail some of the best and brightest examples of branded content. From short, shareable videos to elaborate quizzes, brands really outdid themselves. However, I noticed that most of the experts who compiled "best of" lists cited content that comes directly from brands, not from content studios at publishers. This is a shame! But it is also an opportunity.

Hootsuite—"A Game of Social Thrones"

Hootsuite, the social media management tool, took the opportunity to capitalize on one of the biggest television events of the year. With the fourth season premiere of HBO's *Game of Thrones* looming, Hootsuite created a YouTube video (see Figure 9.9) that played off of the show's opening sequence. The video put Hootsuite at the center of all the most important social media tools, in a map of a

Figure 9.9 A screenshot from Hootsuite's parody of the *Game of Thrones* opening sequence.

sort of social Westeros. This short video capitalized on the popularity of *Game of Thrones*, understanding that many of its young, tech-savvy users would connect and get the joke.

Twixt—WhichAbsurdConsumerPsychographic AreYou.com

If BuzzFeed has taught us anything, it is that people love quizzes. Twixt, an RFP processing app, took advantage of this knowledge and created a website that allows users to figure out which demographic they fit into. This could be dry—or silly—but it's actually quite funny. And as it turns out, I'm a Jenny! Learn all about Jenny (and me) in Figure 9.10. (Unfortunately, the quiz is no longer available online.)

Purina's "Dear Kitten"

If you've used social media in the past year, you've probably seen a "Dear Kitten" video where a wizened old cat schools a kitten in the way of his household (see Figure 9.11). Whether the cat is teaching his new friend about the dog or the way humans behave during the Super Bowl, these videos are adorable, funny, and highly shareable. They also happen to be created in conjunction with BuzzFeed. It's no coincidence that of all the examples I've listed here, this is probably the only one you've heard of unless you're a huge content marketing

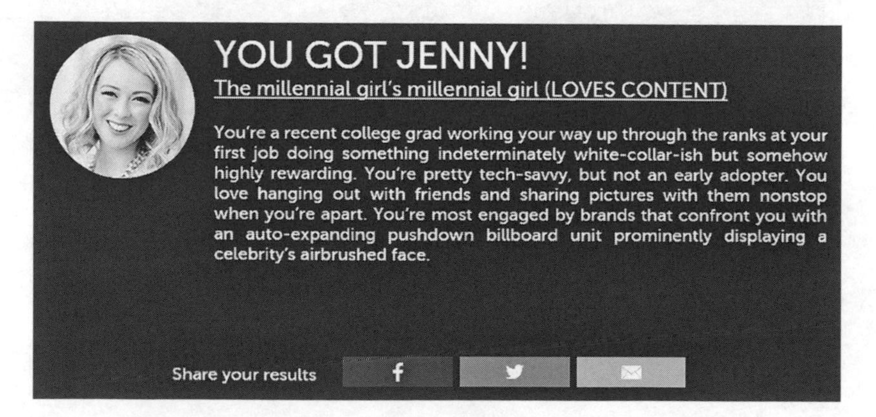

Figure 9.10 A screenshot of results from Twixt's WhichAbsurdConsumerPsychographicAreYou.com.

Figure 9.11 A screenshot from the "Dear Kitten" video series from BuzzFeed and Friskies.

geek. One of the things publishers have to offer branded content clients is their audience, and while Purina's content happens to be especially fantastic, BuzzFeed's massive audience is also to thank for the runaway success of these videos. Word on the street is that one of BuzzFeed's own employees was the voice of the cat—which gives new meaning to "capturing the voice" that audiences love.

Branded Books

Are you wishing there was a *Branded Content for Dummies* book out there? Well, John Wiley & Sons will do you one better. The publisher of the famous "Dummies" series is now creating branded content under the umbrella of its best known brand. Household names such as Google, Coca-Cola, and IBM have already hopped aboard Wiley's branded book bandwagon.

For Google, Wiley created *Connecting People Using Google for Dummies.* The search giant was looking to promote its AdWords product, so the book included a money-off offer. Readers could download the book from a special microsite.

Wiley has created similar branded books about everything from acoustic guitars to happiness (Coca-Cola was behind that one) to green office interiors.

An In-Depth Look at Branded Content

Up until now we've talked about branded content as a means to new revenue for publishers. A big part of that is rendering content creation services, but some really big projects entail a lot more participants than just a client and a media outlet. Following is an *EContent* case study about one such branded content collaboration.

Del Monte Foods: A Case of Thanksgiving Branding

San Francisco-based Del Monte Foods were introduced to American grocery stores in 1886 and have been a pantry staple ever since. "At Del Monte, we will always strive to cultivate the best garden quality vegetables, fruits, and tomatoes to help you and your family live a life full of vitality and enjoyment," according to the company website.

Business Challenge

What would Thanksgiving be without the traditional turkey and a cornucopia of vegetables? In 2014, Del Monte was looking for a way to strengthen its ties to Thanksgiving in customers' minds—specifically as regards its green beans. The company teamed up with PopSugar to implement a content-marketing initiative that included a branded portal for content. Additionally, Del Monte needed assistance with content creation.

Vendor of Choice: Vibrant Media

"Vibrant connects consumers in real time with engaging content and brand experiences—delivered cross platform," says the company website. With solutions for advertisers and publishers, Vibrant places native advertisements across platforms to improve reach and scale. Its clients include Unilever, HP, Microsoft, Jaguar, and Visa.

The Problem in Depth

"With the 2014 holiday season approaching, Del Monte wanted to strengthen ties to Thanksgiving and drive brand interaction and engagement with the famous Del Monte green beans," according to a press release. Virginia Moon, associate brand manager at Del Monte, says, "Del Monte has been around for over 120 years. We're an iconic American brand that people know and love....However, our brand is not very tightly tied to Thanksgiving."

It's hard to compete with the all-important turkey and cranberry sauce for the hearts and minds of Thanksgiving diners. Del Monte wanted its green beans to have a place at the table, so to speak, and decided that a branded content push was the way to go. "We were running our green bean TV ads, which makes a lot of sense in terms of awareness and keeping us top of mind," says Moon. "But to really extend that conversation, create that relevance and that stronger tie to Thanksgiving, we felt we really needed to do something from a digital standpoint—and specifically that content marketing would lend itself to...being able to provide our consumer with something that's extraordinarily valuable to her in the moment—especially during what's a typically stressful holiday occasion."

As any would-be content marketers know, creating great content is hard. Getting it in front of actual potential customers can be even harder. Del Monte does not have an in-house content marketing team. More to the point, the company needed to reach beyond the borders of its own website to reach consumers who were not already immediately thinking about Del Monte when planning their menus. That meant finding the right partners to create branded content that would be sure to keep Del Monte green beans on consumers' minds and then push the content out to a wide audience.

The Solution

With the help of its media-buying agency, Starcom, Del Monte teamed up with Vibrant Media and PopSugar.com to deliver its message. PopSugar describes itself as "a global women's lifestyle brand focused in media, commerce, and technology. Our mission is to connect women with new entertainment, products, and experiences they're most passionate about." This, along with its ability to create a branded portal for Del Monte, made it a great fit for the food provider's Thanksgiving content offensive (see Figure 9.12).

Figure 9.12 A promotional image from Del Monte of its mobile content marketing.

But Del Monte also wanted to increase its reach beyond just that portal, so it also enlisted the help of Vibrant at the suggestion of Starcom. According to Moon, Del Monte was drawn to Vibrant “because of their targeting capabilities—not only through keywords but also through image targeting.”

Vibrant’s Amplify solution can commission, curate, and distribute brands’ paid, owned, and earned content in relevant editorial articles. Del Monte used content created by PopSugar as well as Vibrant to populate its branded portal, which housed the content as well as general lifestyle content related to Thanksgiving that PopSugar was already creating.

Articles contained within the branded site included "Healthy Twists on a Holiday Classic" and "Top Ten Tips for Smart Holiday Entertaining." Writers also offered up their personal green bean casserole recipes. Wyman says that Vibrant works with Scripted, which creates content on demand, to help clients develop the right content. She says they would identify article ideas before briefing "writers on what we want and how we want it to be delivered."

Meanwhile, Del Monte was also creating "data-driven stories for mass-media coverage by partnering with PR Hacker, an agency that specializes in story based, data-driven content that creates news," according to the press release. "For this part of the campaign, Del Monte asked 1,500 Americans to 'go green bean' and rate their fondness for the classic green-bean casserole side dish. The result: The first annual 'Del Monte Green Bean Index'—a ranking of the top 25 U.S. states with the highest concentration of green-bean casserole lovers for the holidays."

While Vibrant helped provide content, it really excelled at leveraging the Del Monte content using Vibrant's contextual ad network that served the branded content up as ads on other sites, says Jennifer Wyman, account executive at Vibrant. So if you happened to be searching around the internet for healthy Thanksgiving recipes last holiday season, there's a good chance Vibrant placed an ad for Del Monte's content within your line of sight. This was made possible through Mosaic, Vibrant's tool that syndicates brand and social content across the web.

The Outcome

The goal of Del Monte's campaign was to drive brand interaction and engagement, and Moon says that, so far, it looks like the campaign was a resounding success. In terms of what Del Monte expected from Vibrant "we were looking for click through rates and time on site" says Moon.

"Click-through-rates were extraordinary," she continues, adding that they "far surpassed industry standards." In addition, she says that time on site was twice the norm. "On average it's something like seven seconds," but with this campaign Del Monte saw time on site jump to almost 15 seconds.

That, Moon says, "speaks to the value of the content and the way Vibrant was able to target" content to the right readers.

According to the press release, "In addition to achieving impressive rates of viral sharing, the Del Monte Green Bean Index was covered on more than 100 media outlets—including top media outlets such as Bloomberg and Yahoo Travel, plus dozens of local TV news stations—garnering an estimated 80 million total audience in less than two weeks."

"What we were able to accomplish with Vibrant was more than what we expected," says Moon. "We were trying to drive value and engagement and that tighter connection with Thanksgiving....If we were to run another digital campaign we would certainly consider working with them again."

Measuring the Results of Branded Content

One of the wonderful things about the web—and specifically digital marketing—is the interactivity. It is easy to know exactly how a digital ad campaign performs, though, that doesn't always hold true for branded content. How is Netflix supposed to know if the *New York Times* piece about female inmates led to more viewers for *Orange Is the New Black*? A UK-based newspaper the *Telegraph*, launched an entire division to answer just this kind of question.

Spark—as the new division is called—aims to give clients more insight into campaigns, which it hopes translates into more confidence in branded content. Ricardo Bilton of Digiday wrote "How the *Telegraph* measures native ad campaigns," which says, "Spark will also offer clients data dashboards for each campaign, which tells them how individual articles are performing in real time."

The *Telegraph* hired a gaggle of data analysts to help make sense of its data for Spark. And it's working. As Bilton wrote, "Data has already influenced how the the *Telegraph* creates sponsored content. In one campaign for coffee company Kenco, the *Telegraph* created a microsite about sustainable coffee in Honduras (see Figure 9.13). But the data showed that only a few hundred readers got to the page by searching for 'sustainable coffee,' instead of finding it while looking for articles about Honduras' issues with drugs

Figure 9.13 A screenshot of the *Telegraph's* content created for coffee company Kenco.

and cocaine. So the *Telegraph* used that data to convince Kenco to let it create content around that topic."

Data is important, but you also have to know what to look for and how to interpret that data—which is why newspapers like the *Telegraph* are spending money on tools and people. According to Brian Honigman's post "7 Metrics to Accurately Measure Your Content Marketing" you need to be looking for

1. Brand lift
2. Increased traffic
3. Social interactions
4. On-Site engagement
5. Lead generation and subscriptions
6. Thought leadership
7. Conversions

If you're a publisher who is still taking those first tentative steps into branded waters, you can't start measuring until you take the plunge. Just remember to figure out what your customer wants to achieve before embarking on a branded-content campaign. You can't be successful if you don't know what you're trying to achieve.

Afterword

Derek Jeter and an Industry in Flux

I researched and wrote *Inside Content Marketing* over the course of about nine months. That is both a long time and the blink of an eye. If you're a pregnant woman, it probably seems like an eternity, but if you're writing a book, it doesn't seem like nearly enough time. Over the course of the summer, fall, and winter, I was totally immersed in the world of content marketing, and when I finally came up for air, I noticed a change. When I first started combing through the annals of content marketing history, it seemed clear that this was a different animal than advertising, as we have known it in the past. But more and more, that line seems to be eroding.

I wrote the sidebar column that follows for *EContent* in 2011. I didn't know it then, but I was dancing around content marketing—and so was the industry.

The Demise of Ad Men

I recently jumped on the *Mad Men* bandwagon. That Jon Hamm sure is handsome, and boy oh boy, did they smoke a lot. There's plenty to gawk at—and cringe at—on that show. The sexism. The debauchery. All those pregnant ladies hitting the bottle and smoking up a storm.

As I watch—floating somewhere between awe and disgust—the goings-on of Sterling Cooper Draper Pryce have got me pondering the modern business of advertising. By the time I was born, Don Draper would have been retired and too old to womanize, but the advertising biz was still in full swing.

I keep thinking about the "Where's the Beef?" lady, Madge hawking her dish soap, and Bartles and Jaymes sitting on their rockers selling wine coolers. Just the other day, I had to explain those old Grey Poupon commercials with the Rolls-Royce to my (much) younger brother.

Lately, I've been enjoying the Allstate "Mayhem" commercials with Dean Winters. You know the ones I'm talking about, where a slightly deranged-looking individual wreaks havoc on property owners. The one where he's a raccoon tearing into an attic makes me laugh every time—and then it makes me wonder what's happening in *my* attic. Last winter, as the snow fell in Connecticut and piled up on my roof, Allstate aired a commercial about a garage collapse, and I started worrying about my own roof and whether mayhem would come crashing through it at any moment. But you'll notice I haven't mentioned changing my insurance carrier.

I appreciate a good advertisement, but I can't think of a single time one has convinced me to run out and buy anything—unless it had a coupon attached. No, I always go for a good deal. A quick look at my inbox is all you need to be convinced that I am a bargain hunter: offers from Travelzoo; 20 percent off of Ann Taylor; free shipping from Cost Plus World Market; double cash back from Ebates. And you better believe there are plenty of offers from Groupon and LivingSocial in my email.

When it comes to commercials, I am an advertiser's nightmare. But if you've got a sale or a coupon, I am your girl. If I like your brand, I'm happy to follow it on Facebook and get whatever deal it is you want to offer me.

Still, as advertising moves further away from the days of Sterling Cooper Draper Pryce, I can't help but lament the loss of something. Social media marketing is great for people like me, but I wonder what will take the place of those iconic brand-building commercials?

I've got a theory, and I imagine you're already seeing it play out at your water cooler—or on Twitter. Instead of

Super Bowl commercials, we'll all be talking about the hot new viral videos in years to come. Heck, we already are!

Remember that YouTube video with robotic-voiced cartoon characters where one was looking for an iPhone and the other was desperately—and rather profanely—trying to convince her that an HTC EVO was a better choice? The salesperson extolled the virtues of the bigger screen, and the buyer asked, "Is it an iPhone?" The salesperson said that no, it wasn't, and the buyer said, "Then I don't care."

The video was a home run on every level. It was hilarious and got into my consciousness. (I still can't say the words "I don't care" without thinking about it.) It got great buzz and made even the most devoted iPhone users wonder if their brand allegiance wasn't a bit silly. It was such a hit that GEICO started using the same free animation tool to produce some of its television spots.

But while I ran around sharing the YouTube video with everyone I thought would be interested, I never once pointed anyone to the GEICO commercial. The traditional advertising guys—the ones in the skyscrapers on Madison Avenue—are playing catch-up with their audience. Sure, sometimes you get a wink and nod that says, "Look we're paying attention." But from Amazon reviews to Groupon, the ad men are losing ground.

Let's face it; we're already looking back on the golden days of advertising with nostalgia—just ask the guy responsible for dusting all the awards in the *Mad Men* office.

As my work on *Inside Content Marketing* came to a close, and I was combing through all the best branded content lists that I mentioned in the last chapter, I came across one list that gave me pause: Joe Lazauskas's "The Best Branded Content of 2014 So Far" for Contently. Lazauskas listed Budweiser's "Puppy Love" ad. You know the one: An adorable puppy and a giant Clydesdale are best of friends (see Figure 10.1), and when the puppy is adopted the Budweiser Clydesdales go to great lengths to stop the new owner from leaving with their friend.

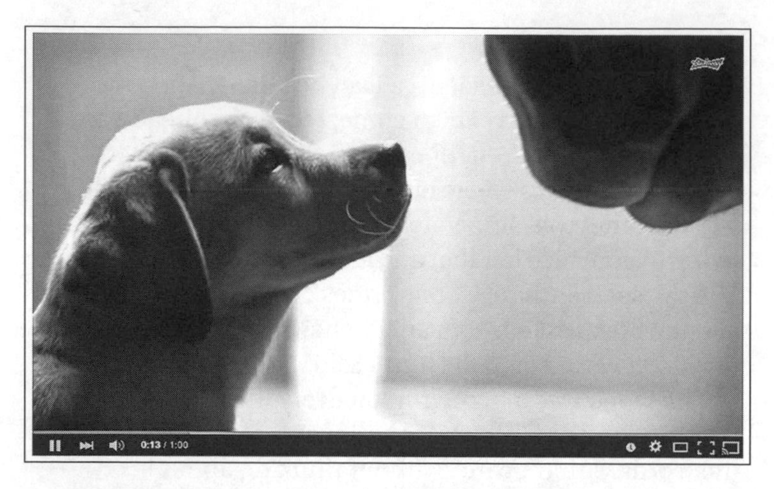

Figure 10.1 A still from Budweiser's "Puppy Love" ad.

Most of you will recognize this as a Super Bowl commercial—not branded content. Or is it? For years people like me, who don't give a hoot about football, have tuned in to the Super Bowl to see the commercials that giant brands have spent millions to develop and place in front of the country's largest viewing audience of the year. What I'd never considered before was how little many of those commercials have to do with the products they are selling. Commercials like "Puppy Love" are all about entertainment and brand awareness. They are about generating word of mouth, and, these days, about getting audiences to share them on the web. In fact, many of them leak on the internet long before game day so that people who don't care about the big game can pass the videos around.

Is it really all that different from content marketing?

It would be easy to say that advertisers are simply taking a page out of the content marketing handbook. Provide your customers with engaging, useful content and they will remember you when it comes time to make a purchase—but Super Bowl commercials were around long before this content marketing renaissance began. It's a real "chicken or the egg" kind of conundrum.

Either way it's clear that content marketing is affecting every facet of the marketing world and is starting to impact the advertising world.

Is Advertising Just Another Form of Content Marketing?

Gone are the days of the *Mad Men* of Madison Avenue. Sad as it is, not only is the midday drinking and smoking gone for good (mostly anyway), but the ads of old are gone as well. Advertising in the 1950s, '60s, and beyond often presented a cheesy, geo-blanketed, retail-heavy message:

"Come on down and save, save, SAVE!"

Today, the game is different. In the world we live in, what I call the "internet maturation phase," we are covered in white noise, mindless drivel from every product seller in the world. We are smothered with ad and logo placements to the point where we tune most of it out. Except for the stuff we REALLY care about.

And that is where the paradigm shift comes into play. Smart advertisers are now focusing on a different form of advertising. And it looks a lot like its marketing brother from another mother, content marketing.

Let me ask you some questions:

Do you remember a time when so many advertisements had deep storylines?

Do you remember a time where the 40-second ad was outdone by the well-done 60-second, even 120-second ad?

It's a new age. It's what I like to call content advertising. It throws out high-frequency 30-second ads which hammer you over the head with loud announcers and endless sales. Now it's about a story. A feeling. A brand wishing to make a connection with us, the consumers.

Before we look at what I believe good content advertising is made of, let's look at some ad examples.

Dodge: God Made a Farmer, "Big Game," 2013

Despite living in beautiful East Tennessee, I am not a farmer. However, this ad made me want to be a farmer and buy a truck. This proved a traditional ad does not need to fit into the typical 30 second box. This two minute ad with the epic 1978 speech by radio broadcaster Paul Harvey was beautiful, and not only did it hit me hard, but I'm sure it hit the target market even harder.

Sam Adams: "For the Love of Beer" (2013)

I'll admit it, this made me want to drink more Sam Adams. Did it have a call to action? No. Did it show a huge URL? No. It showed passionate people working on their passion: beer. It gave us a behind the scenes look at the beer brewing process and what could be better. This did not feel like an ad, it felt like content only. It just happened to take up 30 seconds, and it made this Boston kid want to buy some of his hometown brew again.

Content Advertising is about two things:

The Story. This is not about a pitch. It's about the story behind a product. Content Advertising brings the story to the forefront. Even some of the fictitious stories-like those of a swashbuckling Captain Morgan-get us thinking about how the original purveyors might have intended the product to be enjoyed. The story is everything. If it shines through, you win. If it is diminished by Madison Avenue retail nonsense, you lose. Simple as that.

Being Personal. Let's use Apple as a case study for this. Every ad it puts out could easily be about how wonderful the iPad Air 2 is. But it lets their consumer's personal experiences tell the story instead. In my opinion, that has far more impact.

Products impact us personally. When a brand recognizes this and synthesizes it into an "ad," that's

> where the magic happens. Apple's ads are true. iPads are used for countless purposes in today's connected world and they deeply impact our lives, our health, and our well-being. Showing the stories of people impacted by these devices makes it personal. And when advertising gets down to a personal level, it connects.
>
> Traditional advertising is dead. Content Advertising is alive and well, and the sooner we understand its value and impact, the sooner we content creators and marketers will see our brands thrive.
>
> *Drew Bedard, "The Digital Race" (EContentmag.com)*

Content marketing is changing the game for everyone, even advertisers. The days of Fast Eddy selling you cars at low, low prices are gone. (If your local used-car salesman is still employing this technique, be sure to give him a copy of this book.) These days you're more likely to see a car commercial where a family of dogs are behind the wheel, or a kid dressed like Darth Vader is using The Force on his dad's car.

If you need more evidence that content marketing is taking over, you need look only at Derek Jeter. No need to adjust your reading glasses—I did, in fact, just refer to New York Yankees legend Derek Jeter (as much as it pains my Red Sox soul to do so). When Jeter retired at the end of the 2014 baseball season, people were speculating far and wide about what he would do next. (Personally, I would have taken my piles of money to a beach somewhere.) Which of these sounds most likely to be Jeter's second act? Commentator? Coach?

Content marketer?

If you managed to guess content marketer, I'll assume that it was only because of the context of this book, and not because you are the only person in the world who saw Jeter's next move coming.

Yes, just days after retiring from major league baseball Jeter launched The Players' Tribune. The site is a place for professional athletes to reach out directly to fans by writing their own stories. In "The Start of Something New," the inaugural post on the site, Jeter wrote, "I do think fans deserve more than 'no comments' or 'I don't knows.' Those simple answers have always stemmed from a genuine concern that any statement, any opinion or detail, might be distorted. I have a unique perspective. Many of you saw me after that final home game, when the enormity of the moment hit me. I'm not a robot. Neither are the other athletes who at times might seem unapproachable. We all have emotions. We just need to be sure our thoughts will come across the way we intend."

One might wonder about the wisdom of relying on professional athletes to create your content, but this idea works on so many different content marketing levels, it's almost mind-bending. (I mean, how many publishers can boast Kobe Bryant as an editorial director?) Not only are the athletes/writers marketing their personal brands through the content, Jeter plans to monetize the site through branded content.

It took a few months, but by mid-February of 2015, Jeter announced that Porsche would be signing on as the site's first advertiser (as well as an expansion into other forms of content, like podcasts and Sirius XM radio).

One of the most exciting things about being a part of the media industry—digital and otherwise—is the sense that things are constantly changing. The ground beneath your feet is always shifting. One day stodgy old Rupert Murdoch is the media mogul everyone is talking about, and the next a former Yankee shortstop is coming up with an entirely new concept that may just prove to be the next big disruptive media powerhouse. That is both scary and a wonderful motivation to stay on top of your game and try new things. People and institutions that refuse to change with the times perish. If you have been ignoring how the content marketing revolution is changing your industry thus far, you continue to do so at your own peril. But here's the great thing about content marketers: They love to share what they know! All you have to do is ask.

Ending this book with a content marketing example from the sports world seems apt. After all, who knows more about the importance of building the right team than someone like Derek Jeter? Where would he have been without Alex Rodriguez or Tino Martinez? Would Jeter have been as effective without Joe Torre at the helm, steering the team's strategy? As you go forth and start building your content team, remember that in order to win games, you'll all need to work together.

About the Author

By day, Theresa Cramer is the editor of *EContent*, where she covers the world of digital media and marketing. By night she is a reader and writer of books, NPR addict, and avid gardener. Cramer has over a decade of experience in publishing. From newspapers to books to magazines, she has worked in every arm of the industry. With the inherent curiosity of a journalist, and the attention to detail of a seasoned editor, she helps create content success stories.

A graduate of the University of Connecticut, Cramer began her career working at a small-town newspaper with virtually no web presence. After several years of covering the Board of Education and local sports, she moved on to Harper Collins Publishers. In 2008 she joined the *EContent* team as assistant editor, taking the helm as editor in 2011. Covering the digital media industry has taught Cramer many things, chief among them that the internet allows us all the freedom to experiment but that it takes commitment to strategy and execution to succeed.

Cramer lives in Connecticut with two cats and a dog. She blogs about her adventures in home decorating (and whatever else strikes her fancy) at TheresaCramer.com. Send her your comments at the website or follow her on Twitter @TheresaCramer.

Index